Family Argument

My 20 Years in Yorkshire Cricket

Family Argument

My 20 Years in Yorkshire Cricket

JOHN HAMPSHIRE

Written in association with Don Mosey

London
GEORGE ALLEN & UNWIN
Boston   Sydney

George Allen & Unwin (Publishers) Ltd,
40 Museum Street, London WC1A 1LU, UK

George Allen & Unwin (Publishers) Ltd,
Park Lane, Hemel Hempstead, Herts HP2 4TE, UK

Allen & Unwin Inc.,
9 Winchester Terrace, Winchester, Mass 01890, USA

George Allen & Unwin Australia Pty Ltd,
8 Napier Street, North Sydney, NSW 2060, Australia

First published in 1983

British Library Cataloguing in Publication Data

Hampshire, John
    Family argument.
1. Hampshire, John   2. Cricket players—
Great Britain—Biography
I. Title
796.35′8′0941   GV915.H/
ISBN 0-04-796074-4

Set in 11 on 13 point Plantin by Nene Phototypesetters, Northampton
and printed in Great Britain by Mackays of Chatham

Contents

List of Illustrations

Prologue

On the afternoon of Thursday 27 May 1982, I went out to bat
at Queen's Park, Chesterfield, for Derbyshire against Yorkshire. There was a fairly noisy crowd, excited and excitable as
crowds usually are in the later stages of one-day matches and
there was a little extra undercurrent of excitement at the
appearance of a former Yorkshire captain (and, I like
to think, a 100 per cent Yorkshireman in character) in
opposition for the first time.

There was a little booing from some quarters. Yorkshiremen are not quick to understand, and even less prompt to
forgive, what they rightly or wrongly see as defection. The
realist in me spoke quite clearly: 'You are a professional
cricketer. This is what you do for a living. Derbyshire are
now the county which pay your mortgage. Your job is to do
the best you can for the people who pay you.'

The romantic in me – and there is just a little streak of
romanticism in the most realistic of us – was saying something rather different. It was asking questions which I didn't
want to answer, certainly not at that point. The score was
41 for 2 and Derbyshire still needed to make another 138 to
be sure of a place in the Benson and Hedges Cup quarter-
finals. My old team-mates had received me cordially enough
when we met in the morning, but that was the sociable hour
which is the same on almost any ground in the world before
play begins. We were now involved with the harsh realities of
professionalism out in the middle.

First with Peter Kirsten, then with Geoff Miller, I got on
with the job I was paid to do. Rain and bad light caused a

1

delay and added to the tension. Back we went to the middle and finally a six into the lake which runs along the north side of the ground finished the game with a seven-wickets win for Derbyshire. It was I suppose, a satisfyingly spectacular climax for the spectators and that was what I was there to do – to score runs and entertain the paying customers. And I think most batsmen enjoy hitting sixes.

I didn't particularly enjoy hitting that one. I didn't feel delight or exhilaration at the victory. The Gold Award from Peter Parfitt for my contribution to the win didn't mean as much to me as perhaps it might have done. As a Derbyshire professional I felt professional satisfaction; as a Yorkshire-man, my feelings were quite different.

My father had played his first game for Yorkshire at Queen's Park. I had played my first game for Yorkshire schoolboys there. And I had been called up for my first one as a Yorkshire colt there, too. Here I was, starting yet another phase of my sporting life on the same ground, one of the loveliest in England. It was a significant moment in my career but I could feel no joy in the occasion or the achieve-ment. It would not alter for one second my approach to my new job but as I walked off the field, having played a part in the defeat of Yorkshire, and in my first game against them on a ground which had always been important in my life, I allowed myself the indulgence of an emotional moment – and a feeling of infinite sadness.

1

Yorkshire Born and Bred

Like my father, I was born in the mining village of Thurnscoe in South Yorkshire, beside the great Hickleton Main Colliery. I was a war-time baby, born on 10 February 1941, the eldest of three brothers. The earliest sporting influence in our lives had to come from our father, Jack Hampshire. He was a colliery blacksmith who was taken out of the pits by his own sporting ability. He bowled for Yorkshire in 1937 and went from Mexborough Town to Manchester City at a record fee to play alongside such soccer immortals as Matt Busby, Eric Brook, Alex Herd and Frank Swift. In due course I took up both games and thought myself a better footballer than a cricketer until the time arrived when I had to concentrate on one or the other. Throughout my career I have never regarded myself as a really outstanding cricketer. I have had enough faith in my own ability to make it my career, and I think I have been a rather better player than some who have earned a fair living at the game, but never have I thought I was as good as some other people believed me to be. However, at the time when I had to make a choice, I was, quite frankly, making more money from cricket than I could see any likelihood of making from football so the realistic choice was relatively simple. There will be a school of thought which regards this as a mercenary decision but that philosophy is invariably found

3

amongst those who can afford the luxury of high ideals. When you are considering simple, practical issues of how to make a living, you go for the one which is going to give you the best security and standard of life. Ironically, within a couple of years of my decision, the maximum wage in soccer was abolished and, believing as I did that I was a better footballer than cricketer, it seemed as though I might have missed the boat.

When my father's football career came to end because of a shoulder injury he joined the police force and some of my earliest years were spent at Herringthorpe, still in South Yorkshire. My cricketing life began at the age of five, when a man called Harry Montgomery made me a set of stumps, carved from a single block of wood. My cricket field was the street outside the family home, with the neighbours as my team.

By a simple accident of the grip I applied to the ball on first acquaintance, I developed into a natural leg-spinner and, looking at Yorkshire's traditional aversion to this form of bowling (whether for or against), it is as well that I began to develop my batting! By the time I was seven I was spending hours at the back of the house assiduously trying to perfect a googly and, by way of variation, developing ball-sense by throwing a soft ball against the gable end of the house and catching the rebound. This exercise was a good deal more aesthetically satisfying to the thrower/catcher than it was to the occupant of the house – the incessant thump-thump-thump of the ball against the wall nearly drove my mother mad. These were the starkly austere post-war years; television, with its mixed blessings to Society, had not yet reached the north of England and simply throwing, catching, kicking a ball was a leisure-time luxury to most kids of my age. Idly, we would allow ourselves to dream of playing cricket for Yorkshire; it was the sort of daring, utterly far-fetched dream that brought an almost sensual thrill at the sheer cheek of it – walking out to bat with Hutton, bowling at Compton and Edrich. It was only a dream, but how we loved to indulge ourselves in it.

Then it was down to earth with the more solid business of serving my cricket apprenticeship at Clifton Lane, the home of Rotherham Town Cricket Club, where Sam White was the coach. I got all the encouragement in the world from my father and his mates and from a man called Frank Ellis, who was very close to getting into the Yorkshire side. There were few inviting alternatives to constant practice at Clifton Lane, yet it was not all a matter of bowling and smiting the ball around. These were the days before there was much mechanised equipment and we all did our share of pushing and pulling the lumbering heavy roller up and down next Saturday's wicket. There were a dozen other jobs to be done around the ground as well; membership of a cricket club did not mean merely a week-end of unalloyed delight but the week of preparation which preceded it as well. Family incomes amongst our members did not allow lavish pocket-money and at the end of the day, when the choice was between the bus fare home and the price of a bag of chips, the chips invariably won so the evening's toil was followed by a walk back home. If our extra-mural activities were a little less anti-social than those of some youngsters today, lack of energy was no doubt a contributory factor.

My first bit of cricket folklore – those stories of on-the-field remarks which, as one learns at cricket dinners, the watching public yearn to know about – was bequeathed to me by my father and it came from his first appearance for Yorkshire, against Derbyshire at Chesterfield. His first wicket was 'caught Sellers', one of those close-to-the-wicket specials which were a trademark of Yorkshire in the 'thirties, and as the batsman departed the Great Man sauntered down the wicket and announced, 'Tha'll get no catches like that in t'League, lad.' Thus I first became conscious of the existence of Brian Sellers, a name of which I was to hear a good deal in the future.

In those early teenage years at Clifton Lane the various strands of my cricketing life were beginning to interweave. At Badsley Moor Lane School I made my first acquaintance with a teacher named Charlie Lee, who later became captain of Derbyshire after playing for Yorkshire Colts (and a couple of games for the first team in 1952). Charlie was the man who eventually introduced me to Yorkshire cricket. I went on to High Greave School and from there to Oakwood Technical High School where it all began to happen. Through Charlie Lee I was put under the wing of Cyril Turner, the pre-war Yorkshire all-rounder who later became the county scorer and played an important part in 'bringing on' young players in the South Yorkshire area. Now there seem always to have been two distinct streams of personality in great Yorkshire sides – the stern, unyielding, abrasive, belligerent approach of, say, Wilfred Rhodes, Brian Sellers or Arthur Mitchell, contrasting with the kindly, helpful, almost gentle character-istics of George Hirst or Maurice Leyland, through to Cyril Turner. To be at the county nets in later years with Mitchell and Leyland as coaches was to be involved in the most unbelievable Jekyll and Hyde combination in the history of cricket. When I went to Harrogate for a schools trial, Mitchell and Leyland were the umpires, and I didn't make the final trial because I had been picked primarily as a leg-spinner and a lad called Tony Clarkson (later to play with Somerset) slogged hell out of me. With that black humour which was the nearest 'Ticker' Mitchell ever came to enjoy-ing a joke, he remarked, 'Well, there's one thing about it, lad. Tha's giving it plenty of air.' That was when I decided to work a bit harder on my batting.

At 12, I was a leg-spin bowler who batted no. 11. A couple of years later I graduated to the Rotherham Town second team, still with the same classification, but on my first appearance for the Seconds we had got quite a big score at Monk Bretton and the captain, Albert Morley, offered me promotion to no. 9. I accepted with alacrity and was padded up, eager to bat, when Albert said, 'Wait a minute. Have you got a box on?'

'No,' I replied, 'I haven't got one.'

'Then tha can't bat,' was the final, disappointing, but probably sage adjudication.

So I grabbed the nearest available box, determined not to miss my first chance of batting for the second team, went in at no. 11 after all and got 15 not out. Then, on a dark, evil day with occasional rain, I took 5 for 25 with a wet ball and went home happy.

I played for the first team for the first time when I was 15 and my batting was now coming on. I had an early-morning paper round and one of the houses where I delivered was the home of Charlie Lee, now playing regularly for Derbyshire. Frequently I was in trouble at the paper-shop because I was late in returning: Charlie would regale me with stories of batting against Trueman and Statham and Tyson – 'bruised black and blue from here to breakfast-time' – and it was difficult to tear myself away. These were the names of demi-gods. The possibility of playing with or against them seemed still to be light-years away. Suddenly, it seemed just fractionally less distant when Charlie asked if I had been approached by the county to go to the nets. When I said 'No', he promised, if my father approved, to recommend me. Needless to say, my father approved. By this time I had played for Yorkshire schoolboys at the under-15 level where the competition for that white rose badge was fierce in the extreme. The rising stars of this new generation of Yorkshire cricketers included Jack Birkenshaw, later to play for Yorkshire and Leicestershire and to tour Pakistan, India, West Indies and Sri Lanka with MCC sides, and Duncan Fearnley, who followed his first-class career with

Worcestershire by becoming one of the leading bat-makers in the world.

There was also a boy called Geoffrey Boycott making runs at Hemsworth Grammar School.

2

Through the Gates

My father was never capped by Yorkshire but he did win a 2nd XI cap which was the most sacred object in the family household as I grew up. My grandmother kept it, cherished it, for many years until it subsequently came to rest in my own home. Looking at it as a child, I must have felt the first stirrings of ambition to win one myself and – dare I possibly hope? – perhaps to go one better and wear the full, flowering rose after the cap which carries simply a bud. My imagination was fired, too, by a visit as a seven-year-old to Bramall Lane to watch Don Bradman's Australians, perhaps the greatest touring side of all time: Hassett, Barnes, Miller, Lindwall, Johnston and the young Neil Harvey. 35 years later they are still the names of giants, and in those immediate post-war years when the sporting public flocked to matches, having been starved for so long of top-class spectacle, there was a towering majesty about the game which made an irresistible appeal to my seven-year-old imagination. Ambition, deep-seated and unrecognised, started there.

As a result of Charlie Lee's representations I got my invitation to the Yorkshire nets when I was 16. A half-crown day-return ticket took me from Rotherham (Masborough) station to Leeds, where outside the Post Office I got a bus marked 'Headingley'. When I got off I had no idea where I was or where the ground was. An inquiry revealed that I was about two miles adrift and as I wasn't very big, lugging a damned great cricket bag through the streets of Leeds 6 meant I arrived puffing and panting with the skin chafed from my right leg where the bag continually bumped. So, spotting a little café outside the gates, I decided to have a cup of tea and a bacon sandwich before going to work. Inside was Cyril Turner, who had been coaching me in Rotherham during the two previous winters, with two other chaps in whites. He greeted me in his usual kindly fashion: 'Hello, John. How are you?'

'Fine, thanks, Mr Turner.'

He turned to the other two. 'It's Jack Hampshire's lad.'

The dark, grim-faced member of the trio growled, 'I hope tha can bat bloody better than thi father could.' The roly-poly figure with a cherubic aspect who completed the party contented himself with a little chuckle.

There, in my first proper meeting with the Yorkshire coaches, Arthur Mitchell and Maurice Leyland, I had an immediate and perfect encapsulation of their characters.

The three of them invited me to walk across to the ground with them so my first entrance through the Headingley gates was accomplished in some style. They told me where to get changed, adding, 'Don't forget thi expenses!' This was sound advice from any Yorkshireman to another so I accosted Herbert Walker, the former 2nd XI scorer, who dealt with all expenses. He asked, 'How much is thi train-fare, lad?' and I told him, 'Half-a-crown return and me lunch 'cos it's a long way.'

He looked at me, considered this rather unsubtle suppli-cation and, with the air of one delivering his final offer, announced: 'Ah'll gi' thee one-and-threepence.' So there was my first payment by the Yorkshire County Cricket Club – a total of three-and-ninepence. It had the magic properties of the Rheingeld.

Herbert's enquiry about the fare from Rotherham prompted me to think, 'There can't be many lads here from my part of the county if he doesn't know what it costs,' and I recalled travelling to Rothwell Grammar School for the final schoolboy trial the previous year. I had been struck immediately by the greater confidence of the boys from the central parts of the West Riding. They seemed an entirely different animal from those of us from the south of the county – infinitely more self-assured, as though they were there as a God-given right while the lesser mortals from Sheffield, Rotherham or Doncaster were faced with an eternal struggle to prove themselves. It seemed illogical that wool-textiles and engineering should produce a greater degree of sophistication than steel-rolling and coal-mining but it was something I sensed quite strongly. Perhaps the massive recruitment by Yorkshire over the years from the Bradford League and more refined areas of the Yorkshire League like Leeds and Harrogate had insidiously induced an inferiority complex, I don't know. It may even have affected me, subtly at any rate, in later years, because while some natural accents and uses of the vernacular in the Yorkshire dressing-room became blurred as careers developed, mine have always remained wholesomely – perhaps even aggressively – those of my homeland.

On that afternoon at Headingley in the spring of 1957, the first-team batsmen and senior colt batsmen used the nets first, and then the bowlers padded up. At this point the rest of us were called upon to bowl. My first target was one F. S. Trueman. Now bowling leg-spinners is a fairly complex operation at the best of times. On a cold, miserable April day, when you have been standing around stiffening up for an hour and a half, it can be a trifle difficult. The overhead nets were rather low and my first delivery went straight out, onto the top of the net. I had my first glimpse of the legendary Trueman glare. My second ball bounced nearer my feet than the batsman's and that, too, landed on top of the net. I had my first experience of the legendary Trueman explosion.

11

He turned to Arthur Mitchell and, without any noticeable equivocation, demanded to know what sort of an adjectival so-and-so he had been given to bowl at him.

It wasn't exactly my finest hour. All the same, throughout that session at the nets I was on cloud 9 because looking about me, I could see Appleyard and Wardle bowling, Watson and Lowson batting. It was a glimpse of cricket's Olympus. I remember someone had lost a stud from his boot and it was spotted by Johnny Wardle. He asked me, 'Is that thi stud, lad?' When I said, 'No', he replied, 'Well, tha'd better have it then.' I suppose it was simply his way of telling me to pick it up but I kept that stud for years because Johnny Wardle had 'given' it to me.

By the following year I had left school and, on the advice of my father, decided to concentrate on cricket as my major sport and to learn a trade as a safeguard – something to fall back on if the impossible happened and cricket for some reason unimagined could not be my life. I became an apprentice in the printing trade which meant having to ask for time off work every time I went to the nets. It meant getting up at the crack of dawn, walking to the station (no money for taxi-fares) and taking the train to Leeds. In winter, it meant rushing home from work, scrubbing the ink off my hands, dashing down to the station, arriving at Headingley feeling absolutely knackered. Sometimes the nets were at Bramall Lane – a rattling, bone-shaking tram-ride to Sheffield. Sometimes you didn't even get a bowl and just now and again you permitted yourself the ultimate heresy of asking yourself, 'What the hell is it all about? Why am I going through all this?' And you knew the answer: as long as the invitations kept coming, so long would you keep going to Headingley because somehow, some day, you might be asked to play cricket for Yorkshire. Those days are not exactly ancient history, but looking at attitudes today, it does seem a very, very long time ago.

In my second year at the Yorkshire nets I was picked for the Yorkshire Federation team (effectively the county's third team), which plays a series of games during the schools' summer holidays. I left home at 6 am to get to Baildon, which is roughly 50 miles from my home. In 1983 it sounds a very simple matter to travel that distance but in 1958, with no family car, no friends who owned a car available to take me, no-one living locally who was also picked to play, it became the worst nightmare journey of my life. The hours ticked by as I rode on a bus to the station, the train to Leeds, another train to Bradford, a search for the bus station and a service to Baildon. I arrived an hour late, an hour which was spent in an agony of frustration and terror. Would I have been left out of the side? If so, would I ever be picked again? Was this the end of my career before it had begun? I willed the train to go faster, prayed there would be no-one wanting to board the bus at each stop. I would have liked to cry. My own sense of discipline which, importantly in my book, involves punctuality, was outraged. But even transcending that was the awful, sickening fear that I had missed the game altogether.

Mercifully, we were fielding when I reached Baildon, and (I bless the man who made the decision) the substitute fieldsman was pulled off for me to take his place. After a couple of overs it rained and there was no further play, but I had got my Yorkshire Federation cap. The following year there was a Federation tour of Midlands counties, and with me in that party was a youth called Geoffrey Boycott.

3
Under the White Rosebud

Those early days at the Headingley nets may not have brought about a spectacular advancement in my career with Yorkshire but they certainly had a marked effect upon my progress with Rotherham Town. My batting was now developing into a very useful part of my game and I had one long session in the nets to the bowling of Appleyard and Wardle. I was a 16-year-old Rotherham second-teamer at the time but in that whole session, to two of the greatest bowlers Yorkshire have ever had, I didn't get out. I went back home telling myself that if those two couldn't dismiss me, then no-one in Barnsley's 2nd XI (our opponents the following Saturday) was going to have my wicket. I must have believed myself because when Saturday came I carried my bat through the innings for 90 not out! That got me into the Rotherham first team and I never left it until I played for Yorkshire in 1961. Those local derby matches with Barnsley usually produced something interesting. One year (again a 2nd XI fixture), I left my bat on the team bus and had to borrow one from another member of the side. I got some runs with it and a reporter on the *Barnsley Chronicle*, who played for Barnsley seconds against us, said he'd like to write a little story for his paper about the youngster who got runs with a borrowed bat. The reporter was Michael Parkinson.

There seemed to be hundreds of young cricketers in the

14

dressing rooms at those Yorkshire nets and I wonder how many sat down from time to time and wondered, 'How am I going to break through this opposition?' The first team were re-building with young players like Bryan Stott, Ken Taylor, Philip Sharpe, Brian Bolus and Don Wilson to reinforce established men like Close, Illingworth, Padgett, Trueman and Binks. Waiting in the wings were more senior Colts like Dickie Bird, Jack Birkenshaw and Duncan Fearnley. And, so it seemed to us, behind them stood literally scores of youngsters of 15, 16 and 17, aching for a chance, all with lots of ability. Some fell by the wayside, some gave it up and went off to other counties, some stuck it out, waiting for the Call. I very nearly joined the emigrants myself for, despite my burning ambition to be a Yorkshire player, it seemed absolutely hopeless when I looked at the massed ranks of real ability which stood between me and the top.

Jack Birkenshaw, Duncan Fearnley and I had been told at the schoolboy level that there would be a job for us with Northamptonshire if we ever decided to move on. Then, with the Federation, I got a big hundred at Edgbaston. In due course this led Tom Dollery to invite me, over lunch, to sign a contract with Warwickshire. I think I might well have accepted the offer, but Yorkshire refused to release me and there at last I had the first, faint intimation that there might be a career for me on the lines I had dreamed about for so long. But I honestly couldn't see where the opening was going to appear, and life was beginning to get a little compli-cated. Yorkshire have never had a ground staff as such so there was no way I could be paid unless I played for one of the sides. So it was necessary to keep a job simply because I had to have some source of income, and that meant either asking for time off or taking holiday (often at times inconvenient to my employers) when called up to play. It was a very tricky situation. Then, in the third week of May 1959, the Great Call came. It came in the form of a printed postcard from county headquarters in Leeds and it read: 'You are invited to play for Yorkshire II v Derbyshire II at Chesterfield on 27th and 28th May.' That was the most glorious piece of prose I had ever read in my life. Quite apart from my personal delight, I have always cherished the wording of such cricket communications: 'You are *invited* . . .' No demands, no peremptory instructions. It's the same from Colts cricket right up to Test level, a courteous invitation. Just one of a number of things which separates cricket from so many other sports.

I think my father was more chuffed than I was, if that was possible, especially as he had made his start at Queen's Park, so he went down with me. I was glad that he felt so happy, and then there was the match fee of £6! At the same time I was delighted to be chosen as a South Yorkshireman. It had seemed to me for a long time that with the notable exception of F. S. Trueman, not many lads from 'my' territory broke through to the county side. There were some on the fringe – Eric Burgin, the Kettleborough cousins – but very few seemed to get firmly established. It didn't occur to me for a minute that, far from being established myself, I had just been called up for my first 2nd XI game. All I could think was, 'This is it. You've cracked it.'

I reported to Ted Lester, the captain, and was told I was twelfth man.

No blow in the box from any fast bowler has ever made a bigger impact. I had never even thought about that possibility. My father's disappointment was, if anything, even greater and as we watched the game start he grumbled, 'How the hell does Sharpie get to first slip, a bloody junior pro?' We weren't, of course, to know that P. J. Sharpe would become probably the greatest slip-fielder in the world. If my disappointment had been less crushing, I might perhaps have spared a thought for Dickie Bird, now the prince of umpires but then a colts batsman of great application and patience. 48 hours before arriving at Chesterfield he had scored 181 not out for Yorkshire in the Championship against Glamorgan at Bradford and when the game finished before lunch on the third day he must have thought that he had cracked it for all time. But no – it was back to the salt mines for H. D. Bird and there he was next day, with the second team in Chesterfield. There is a popular legend in some circles that Dickie Bird is the man who got 181 not out and never played for Yorkshire again. It's not quite true, because Dickie played nine more County Championship innings that season, plus a two-day match in Ireland and one first-class game at the Scarborough Festival. At the end of the 1959 season Yorkshire released him and Leicestershire signed him. If I hadn't been feeling so sorry for myself that May morning I might have spared a sympathetic thought for Harold Dennis Bird – a South Yorkshireman, too!

If there was a lesson to be learned from those events it was a pretty obvious one: the lesson of humility. The first thing a Yorkshire professional had to understand was that he was part of something which was very big indeed – so big that no Test player, no matter how many caps he possessed, was anything more than just another player when he rejoined his county. When players stopped learning that truth, the deterioration of Yorkshire cricket, after more than 100 years of eminence, began.

But such philosophical thoughts were far from my mind as I performed the twelfth man's duties at Queen's Park on 27 May 1959. I stayed the night with the team, even though it was only about half-an-hour's run from my home to Queen's Park, and some of my disappointment oozed away as I sampled for the first time the experience of staying overnight with a Yorkshire team.

By the end of the game my frustration had just about gone and I could start looking forward to my next 'invitation' which was, in fact, for a second-team match at Edgbaston a mere two days later. This time I played, but not with conspicuous success: opening with Brian Bolus, I was run out for 14, and lbw to Jack Bannister for 13. One thing I had completely forgotten about until I looked up the match details was: 'B. T. Glynn, b Hampshire, 28'. By this time I was a batsman who could bowl leg-spinners and, in the Yorkshire tradition, I couldn't really expect to find much employment in the secondary branch of my trade. Still, there were my first bowling figures at county 2nd XI level: 4–0–23–1. I don't know who B. T. Glynn is or was but, bless him, he's a part of my life.

Against Northamptonshire II I hit 61 and 22, against Durham 48, against Northumberland 21 and against Cumberland 24 and 0: 203 runs in eight innings. It didn't suggest I was going to be another Bradman, but then I didn't think so, either. During the month of July a young man called Geoffrey Boycott played two games with the Colts.

4

The First Lesson

The year 1960 was one of entrenchment and by the end of it I was an established 2nd XI player. The senior side was still basically a young team with a pool of good players, especially batsmen, and that was the main stumbling-block to any more progress. By now, from being a leg-spinner who batted a bit I had graduated through the phase where I was a batsman who bowled leggers, to the status of an opening batsman who rarely bowled at all and then only on occasions when we were heading for a certain draw or in a pointless situation. In 1960 I bowled just seven overs for the Colts (0–14) but I batted 23 times, scoring 793 runs which was just a few more than my nearest rival, Chris Balderstone. My first century in Minor Counties cricket came at Jesmond in June, when my 120 was part of an opening stand of 265 with Bryan Stott. At Whitsuntide I had my first taste of Roses cricket – or rather Rosebuds – at Old Trafford where I shared an opening partnership of 145 with Philip Sharpe. Lancashire included men like Brian Booth (later to go to Leicestershire and a player with whom I shared certain fellow-feelings as an opening batsman/leg-spinner), Jackie Bond, Malcolm Hilton, Harry Pilling and Roy Tattersall. Hilton, a man who had dismissed Bradman; Tattersall, who had had an Australian tour with England! So scores of 68 and 20 were worth having in the personal record-book. The name of G. Boycott did not cross my horizons in 1960 at all and to tell you the honest truth I did not notice this any more than I had noticed him when he was around. Of course I was conscious that he was there as a fellow-member of the team, but Boycott was always a quiet, studious sort of individual, very much given to keeping himself to himself, whereas I had always been a pretty good mixer and I was always anxious to be in a crowd who wanted to talk cricket and to have a drink and a laugh. Boycott was someone I vaguely knew and that was all. It was only many years later, and completely to my surprise, that I learned that *he* was extremely aware of *me*. I regarded myself as one of a group of young players who were all rivals for places in the first team when the Call came; some were perhaps a bit more advanced than me and some, I felt, were a little further down the scale. Jack Birkenshaw had always seemed first favourite since our schoolboy days and Duncan Fearnley was very highly thought of as well.

There was always tremendous rivalry between all of us but not, I think, any animosity. So I was staggered to learn that through all those early years Geoff Boycott had watched my progress with a rather personal scrutiny. True, I had got to the Yorkshire nets first, and then into the Colts before he did. In 1961 I was to get a chance with the first team while Geoff had to wait until 1962. But these were coincidental matters which never occurred to me. In fact it was only in 1982 that I was told for the first time how Boycott, often near to tears and sometimes actually in tears during those early 'sixties, used to say, 'They think Jack Hampshire's a better player than me, but I'll show 'em, I'll show 'em.' And he did, too – no-one's going to deny that. But I have already said that I have never regarded myself as being as good a player as other people thought me to be. Indeed, it was very difficult indeed to think particularly highly of oneself on joining that vast array of talent which Yorkshire could field in the early 'sixties. The first lesson one learned was humility.

So there was no thought of Geoffrey Boycott, or why he had been missing from the Colts in the season of 1960, as I entered the following season. The greatest moment of my life up to that point came during the game at Ashington, against Northumberland, when our captain, Ted Lester, told three of us – Peter Kippax (a leg-spinner/batsman!), Tony Hatton (a pace bowler) and myself – 'You three have to join the first team at Brighton tomorrow.' We were needed because Brian Close and Freddie Trueman were in the England side playing Australia in the fourth Test at Old Trafford, a famous Test in which Davidson and McKenzie held up England with a last-wicket stand on the final morning and then Richie Benaud, that very shrewd captain, bowled his leg-spinners round the wicket, pitching into the bowler's rough. It was a fascinating and highly effective piece of theory and Close (never a slouch when it came to cricket theory) adopted counter-measures of his own which were theoretically sound but which did not look so good in practice. So while a lot of notable batsmen failed on that occasion, criticism for the defeat was heaped almost exclusively upon the head of D. B. Close. In some ways he was born to be a martyr!

When Ted Lester dropped his bombshell on three excited young men, there was a period of rather prolonged rejoicing. Then, damn it, a serious practical difficulty reared its ugly head: Ashington is 20 miles or so north of Newcastle-upon-Tyne; Brighton is 60-odd miles south of London. And not one of us had a car. It was Peter Kippax's father who came up with the idea of flying south, and so it all became a great adventure because none of us was exactly a veteran of air travel. We got a plane from Newcastle Airport to London, a bus into Victoria, a train to Brighton – and arrived before the big boys who had travelled down from a game at Headingley. We reported to the captain (Vic Wilson), bright-eyed and eager. He told Kippax and Hatton that they were in the team. And guess who was twelfth man?

After making that long journey south in a state of euphoric excitement, the feelings of anti-climax and disappointment were bitter indeed, especially as the other two were playing. Richard Langridge made his first century in the Sussex innings and his big stand with Les Lenham meant that I spent a long time sitting up on the balcony with men who up to that point had been just names in *Wisden* and the newspapers to me: Jim Parks, Ian Thomson, Kenny Suttle, Don Smith. That was some compensation for me, but to tell the truth I was a little disenchanted with life as we moved on to the next Championship game at Leicester. Now, until I saw him injecting himself on the first morning of the Sussex match, in the little room that I shared with him and Peter Kippax on the top floor of the hotel, I had no idea that Tony Hatton was a diabetic, but I do know that at the end of that game he was absolutely shattered. That was really why I made my first-team debut at Leicester in his place.

We fielded first as Leicestershire scored 255 and the only clear recollection I have of that time, in the field for Yorkshire for the first time, was when a ball was hit high into the air towards my part of the field. I was (and still am to this day) satisfied that it wasn't a catch; there was no way I could have got to it. So I moved in to take it on the bounce and Ray Illingworth, the bowler, told me I ought to have made more of an effort to catch it. I wasn't to know at that stage that in his early days with Yorkshire, Ray had experienced a good deal of that sort of critical comment from Bob Appleyard to the extent that he used to dread the ball coming anywhere near him. The first lesson is humility.

The complaint did nothing to induce peace of mind, and when Yorkshire batted I went to sit for a while with my parents, who had driven down to watch the game along with Judy, the girl who was to become my wife. It wasn't long before my father said, 'Don't you think you ought to go and get some pads on?' I roused myself from brooding reverie to find that Terry Spencer and Brian Boshier were wreaking a certain amount of havoc. It wasn't a bad batting line-up with

Vic Wilson at no. 8, but those two were seaming and swinging it all over the place. We were 40 for 5 when J. H. Hampshire walked to the wicket as a Yorkshire batsman for the first time.

Quite honestly, I don't remember much about it beyond the fact that the cricket had a quality I had never experienced in my life. I got 11, one of only four batsmen to reach double figures, feeling all the time that I was out of context with the whole game. I suppose I wasn't the first, or the last, cricketer to ask himself: 'What the hell am I doing here? It's a whole new game.' But I felt very strongly that I wasn't a good enough player to be out there. Was this what all my years of practice and hope and yearning had been about? Was this why I had got up at the crack of dawn to go to Headingley and Sheffield? Was this why I had dashed to the nets after a day's work, scrubbing the printer's ink from my hands and tearing off on the bus or the tram or the train? I was overwhelmed by a sense of my own inadequacy. I felt a million miles out of my class. It was, of course, a personal thing. I had never been a particularly self-confident individual but what I had been able to do well in life was to play ball-games. Here, plunging suddenly into a higher sphere of just that sort of activity, I felt I had been tried and found wanting. My natural lack of confidence in everyday life now took over and submerged that degree of faith which, up to that point, I had never questioned so far as my cricketing ability was concerned. It was a sobering, in some ways a depressing moment.

We were bowled out for 101 and set a target of 383 to win. This time I went in at 96 for 5! With Doug Padgett I put on 96 for the sixth wicket and, after getting an individual 61 in my second Championship innings, I was lbw to the off-spinner, John Savage, who later became coach at Lancashire. I went back to that rickety old pavilion at Grace Road (before the whole face of Leicestershire cricket was transformed by Mike Turner as the manager there) feeling absolutely shattered. The physical effort had been considerable, but much more exhausting was the degree of concentration required – far greater than anything I had ever known at that time. But at least some of my cricketing confidence had returned; at least, I thought, I am not quite such a modestly gifted player as I thought I was 24 hours ago, at least I have proved to myself that I can get runs at this level. It never occurred to me that I might not have proved it to others. I reached the dressing room to the plaudits of my more ex-perienced team-mates for Yorkshire's newest batsman: 'What a bloody awful shot to get out to.' Verily, the first lesson in Yorkshire is humility.

To emphasise the point, I was despatched to join the Colts for their game against Cheshire, never to return to the 1st XI that season or, as far as I could then ascertain, ever again. In the game at Stalybridge, I was bowled by Freddie Millett (Mr Cheshire Cricket himself and one of the great characters of Minor Counties) for 1. But the season was not entirely one of disillusion. On 17 and 18 July the Colts met a side of young visiting South Africans under the name of the Fezela XI at Scarborough. They were sponsored by that fine sporting benefactor, Wilf Isaacs, and they included men who were to make a marked impact upon international cricket until politics sealed them off from the Test arena: Barlow, Peter Pollock, McLean, Lindsay, Van der Merwe, Botten, Elgie and Colin Bland, who raised cover-point fielding to an art form and entertainment in itself. My first encounter with the pace of Peter Pollock was to be bowled for 0 and to find my 28 in the second innings was the top score. So absorbed were the South Africans in every aspect of the game that a throwing contest was staged at the end of a day's play. I had a pretty good 'arm' and was reasonably pleased with a throw from in front of the pavilion at Scarborough, first-bounce into the seats at the Trafalgar Square end of the ground. Colin Bland then threw one into that stand full pitch, without a bounce.

24

This was the man who practised for hours picking the ball up on the run and firing it in at one stump. It was the sort of cover-point fielding the world had not seen since the days of Learie Constantine and it helped to raise the standards of outcricket everywhere.

In September, I was picked for the Minor Counties XI to play the touring Australians at Jesmond. It was a ground which had happy memories for me because I had made my maiden 2nd XI century there, and the match brought me into direct contact with one of those heroic figures I had seen at Bramall Lane when I was seven years old – Neil Harvey. He captained the Australians in the game and in fact took my wicket in the first innings. Wisden recorded: 'Two fine innings [129 and 54] by Hampshire, a Yorkshire colt, marked this entertaining match in which the bat generally mastered the ball. Hitting three sixes and sixteen fours, Hampshire made his 129 in three hours.' I found the Australians a friendly bunch, especially the great Harvey, Barry Jarman and that fine wicket-keeper, Wally Grout, so in one way the season ended on a happy note. Not, though, in the context of Yorkshire cricket: looking back on my visits to Hove and Leicester, at the apparently cavalier attitude of Authority in my native county, and at the quality of the competition for places, I could see very little future for me there. Once again I applied for my release and once again it was refused.

So, short of spending time qualifying for another county (and to an impatient 20-year-old who wanted everything to happen now, that seemed a terrible waste of time), I had to content myself with waiting to see what happened next. For me, nothing very exciting did happen at the start of the 1962 season with the Colts, and when a colts batsman was called up to join the 1st XI for a three-match 'tour' against the touring Pakistanis at Bradford, Northants at Northampton and Derbyshire at Chesterfield, the man they sent for was not J. H. Hampshire but G. Boycott. He got 4 and 4 against the tourists, 6 and 21 not out at Northampton, 47 and 30 not out against Derbyshire. He was not one of the rivals I had felt I had to contend with in my fight for first-team status. There were enough of those in Bolus, Sharpe, Stott, Taylor, to add to established names like Padgett, Close, Illingworth, to make life difficult without having to worry about contemporaries starting the new season with a glut of big scores as Boycott had done. Now there came another consideration. In a gradual sort of way, I had settled as a no. 4 batsman with the Colts. I liked the position better because I had never considered my technique good enough against the new ball, especially in the hands of men I might encounter in first-team cricket, and there was in those days a certain specific requirement attached to each place in the batting order. Openers, naturally enough, had to be good players of fast bowling with the shine on the ball; no. 3 had to be a man of high-class technique in case an opener went quickly; no. 4 was traditionally the stroke-maker on the assumption that the innings would be established by the time he went in to bat. I had always enjoyed hitting the ball hard and I felt no. 4 was right for me. But the first team seemed undecided on the best opening pair. They had tried Bolus and Taylor, Stott and Taylor, Padgett and Stott, Boycott and Padgett. It looked as though a colts opener might have a better chance to establish himself in the senior team than a no. 4 for whom there was an abundance of rivals amongst the more experienced stroke-makers in Yorkshire's ranks. Had I missed the boat by changing my role? The doubts came flooding back. Was I really good enough to force my way in by the quality of my batting? Was my technique good enough to stand up to the bowling that was around then? Was I ever going to get a spell in the first team which would be long enough to allow me to answer these questions both to myself and the county selectors?

When the chance came to answer them it came in an un-expected way. By July I had started to get a few runs for the Colts and on 15 July, in the middle of a week-end game against Northants at Bramall Lane, some of the Yorkshire team went across to Colwyn Bay to play in a one-day match for Freddie Trueman's benefit. I joined them and got a hundred which didn't mean a great deal in its own particular context. But it was against reasonable opposition and at the end of the day Ronnie Burnet, who had led Yorkshire out of the wilderness in 1959 and was now a committee man, took me on one side. 'For God's sake, don't put in any more requests for your release,' he said. 'I think you'll be getting a chance pretty soon.' Obviously my attempts to move on had been remembered and had not done me a great deal of good; it was, I suppose, the ultimate heresy in the eyes of the York-shire committee. But when I returned home to Rotherham that evening my mother said a telegram had arrived, asking me to phone the Yorkshire secretary, John Nash, urgently. I went to the telephone box across the road to call him. His message was: 'Report to Headingley on Wednesday for the game against Notts.' I duly reported, I wasn't made twelfth man, I batted at no. 6 above men like Ray Illingworth and Vic Wilson, the captain. And I scored two in a total of 441 for 9 declared!

Once again a sense of failure overwhelmed me. All the doubts returned. I still didn't believe in myself sufficiently to feel I should be there as of right. I knew that I desperately, obsessively, yearned to be a Yorkshire cricketer but when-ever I looked like realising that ambition I was immediately assailed by doubts. I'm sure it happens to other players. I've no doubt it afflicts young golfers who are confident in their ability to play strokes – until they find themselves in the suffocating atmosphere of tournament competition with great names all around them. It is no longer them against the course: there are hidden pressures lurking everywhere which

are apparent to no-one else, except those who have been
through that sort of experience. Perhaps it was something of
that sort with me, because on 19 July 1962 I was asking
myself if I had 'blown it' once more. But help was on its way,
this time in the form of divine intervention – and I'll bet
F. S. Trueman has never thought of himself in that context!

Now I had been called up for that game against Notts
because Fred and Philip Sharpe had gone to Lords for the
last-ever Gents v. Players match in which FS was captain of
the mercenaries. Despite my undistinguished performance
at Headingley, I was retained in the Yorkshire party but I
could not realistically expect to play in the next game at
Taunton with Sharpie back from Lords. Saturday morning
in Taunton dawned bright and fair and I awaited the call
from the captain which would announce that I was twelfth
man. In the dressing room the assembled throng was
noticeably in two groups, with the senior pros like Close,
Illingworth and Binks gathered around the captain and more
junior personnel like Don Wilson, Tony Nicholson and Mel
Ryan in another corner. I joined the latter group and we
heard the whispered consultations rising in volume. Vic's
voice argued, 'I'm leaving him out.' Matters of high moment
were clearly under discussion and it was no place for junior
pros. We hastily departed in search of nets but not before we
had noticed that one distinguished figure was missing from
the hierarchy – that of F. S. Trueman, fast bowler extra-
ordinary. Fred had driven down from London with Sharpie,
arriving in the early hours, and regarded himself as entitled
to a lie-in instead of reporting to the ground one hour before
start of play which was the unwritten but clearly understood
drill on the first morning of a match. We discovered that the
nets were unfit because of overnight rain, so uncertainly we
inched our way back into the dressing room. FS had now
risen from his bed, put in his appearance at the ground something less than half-an-hour before play was due to begin and

28

been told by the captain, 'You're late, so I'm dropping you from the side.' The man who took 122 wickets for Yorkshire that season and another 22 for England, who had skippered the Players against the Gents, who was my greatest, the ultimate, hero, was clearly taken aback. Instead of the nuclear explosion we all anticipated, his reaction was strangely and uncharacteristically mild: 'All right, sunshine. If that's the way you want it, that's it.' Later that day, when Fred had consumed a pint or two of consolation, he expressed himself a little more forcefully to anyone inclined to listen, but the shock of being dropped, I'm sure, had a delayed-action effect.

The great, the one-and-only FST had been dropped and disciplined! I watched the proceedings in wide-eyed, incredulous wonderment. He was ordered to return home at once and to present himself before the Yorkshire committee the following Tuesday morning. He sublimated the dawning sense of outrage by staying another night and a day in Taunton before heading for Leeds to receive his reprimand, then went off to Trent Bridge to knock hell out of the Pakistanis in the fourth Test by way of working off his resentment. He rejoined us, still larger than life, at Middlesbrough the following week when he knocked a little bit of hell out of Kent as well. I am glad he was not in Taunton to see Peter Wight, who lived in mortal fear of Trueman's bowling and never scored runs against Yorkshire, gleefully pile up 215 against a Trueman-less attack.

I took Fred's place in the Yorkshire XI in that game against Somerset, stayed in the side for the remainder of the 1962 season and was batting with Bryan Stott at Harrogate on 7 September when we won the game by seven wickets – and the County Championship. Who knows what course my life might have taken if Fred had not decided to have an extra hour in bed on that July morning? I did not measure the extent of divine intervention as I played – with a marked absence of distinction – in that game against Somerset. But since then I have thought about it many, many times. It marked the beginning of the happiest days of my life.

5

On the Road with FST

Life for the professional of the 1980s is a bit of a nightmare of
rushing up and down motorways and the complexities of a
fixture list which has you playing a County Championship
match at, say, Chesterfield on Saturday, Monday and
Tuesday, but having to drive to, perhaps, Southampton for
the John Player League game on the Sunday. Now there are
obvious dangers in these high-speed dashes at the end of a
tiring day in the field or after playing a long innings, and I
marvel that there have not been more serious accidents to
cricketers. In the 'sixties, it was an entirely different matter
because Sunday cricket had not arrived and that was a
glorious day of rest for those who simply wanted to put their
feet up, or a day of intense competition, but always laced
with laughter, on the golf course. Sunday was the county
cricketer's traditional golf day and we had reason to be very
grateful indeed to the many clubs, up and down the country,
who gave us the courtesy of the course without hesitation.
In the Yorkshire side we had good golfers like Brian Close
and Ken Taylor who usually fixed up highly competitive
fours with whatever 'tigers' were available amongst the
opposition or the host golf club; we had the not-so-good
like myself, Mel Ryan, Tony Nicholson, Philip Sharpe; and
we had the enthusiastic-but-no-earthly-use-at-all amongst
players who came into the side from time to time. One of

31

these was an engaging character called David Middlewood (known as 'Cowboy'), a fast bowler from Hull, who asked to join a group of us at the Brass Castle Club, Middlesbrough, one Sunday afternoon, insisting that he had played the game and knew the rudiments of golf etiquette. We were a bit doubtful, but not prepared to be so inhospitable as to leave him on his own, so he joined Sharpe, Nicholson and myself on the first tee, where he started with three fresh-air shots. Worse, he didn't seem to find it a cause for any concern that as we made a rather laborious progress down the first fairway we were causing a serious hold-up of club members waiting to tee off behind us. It was becoming a bit embarrassing so the other three of us hurried onto the green, putted out and were just replacing the flag when Cowboy finally arrived. We patiently pulled out the flag for him to sink the ball and announce with a complacent smile, 'That's a four. What did everybody else get?'

Tony Nicholson, never one to suffer fools gladly, exploded, 'You pillock, Cowboy. You were four when you got off the bloody tee and you must have had another ten since then.'

Cowboy turned to face his accuser, breast heaving with righteous indignation: 'Nay damn. You don't count it when I don't hit the ball, do you?'

There was nothing more to be said after that. The three of us carried on our own game with the Cowboy happily hedging and ditching his way around the far-flung outposts of the course, but there was one final item to be passed on to the rest of the team over a pint that evening. One of our press corps, who had driven up to the course to watch the various contests, observed Mr Middlewood in the middle of an uncut hayfield on the left of the seventeenth fairway. He was a good 50 yards out of bounds and addressing the ball (obscured to the observer by the prime, knee-deep grass). Looking up in search of some badly needed advice, he spotted the newspaperman and hollered, 'Hey, Don, am I all right with a 2-iron here?'

They were happy days, but even then there were some exhausting car-journeys: Bradford to Swansea, Taunton to Northampton, Clacton to Scarborough. They seem daunting enough now, but those were the days when most motorways existed only on the drawing-boards of civil engineers. And just about 75 per cent of those journeys involved passing through Birmingham – not the streamlined Brum of today, its fine centre of modern buildings slashed with urban free-ways, but the Brum of traffic snarl-ups in the Bull Ring, the Brum with a so-called ring-road which threaded a zig-zag path around suburbia with a marked lack of direction signs. The story went round the circuit that a Gloucestershire player of rural antecedents got hopelessly lost on a trip through Birmingham to Derby and stopped to ask a parked motorist for help. The chap looked at him with despairing eyes and replied, 'Don't ask me, mate. I've been trying to get off this bloody ring-road since VJ Day.'

They were wearisome trips, but in their way they helped to cement friendships between pairs of players who habitually travelled together, and they contributed richly to the folklore of cricket. It was a pretty safe bet that as we joined the opposition for a pre-match cup of tea each Saturday and Wednesday morning, someone would have a new tale of exotic adventures on the by-roads of England. Some of them have gone into the repertoire for evermore, like a trip made by Ray Illingworth and the gloriously, incomparably vague Richard Hutton from Clacton to Scarborough. No-one was in a particularly happy frame of mind because Trevor Bailey had made a draw of it in Clacton with one of those infamous head-down batting performances which had (as ever) frus-trated all attempts to dislodge him. Everyone was tired, con-scious that vital points had gone down the drain, and every point was vital to Yorkshire in every match because we were

quite simply expected to win the Championship every year or
our chairman, our committee and our members would most
certainly want to know the reason why. So Illy drove through
Essex and Cambridgeshire to the Norman Cross on the A1,
knowing that he could get his head down on the second half
of the journey. After a snack at the hotel, Richard took over
the driving and before too long, in fact the Grantham rounda-
bout, Illy heard those immortal words: 'I say, Raymond,
don't your brakes work?' He awoke and, in his own bitter
recollection, 'with the bloody awful smell of burning rubber
filling the car' his new Zodiac was approaching the rounda-
bout at something like 60 miles an hour. Richard had driven
from the Norman Cross with the handbrake on! It was not
easy to persuade the motor engineers of rural Lincolnshire at
ten o'clock at night that a new braking system was a matter
of the direct urgency. Yorkshire's acting captain and his
co-driver, still locked in mutual recrimination, arrived in
Scarborough at 2 am. Next morning Illy lost the toss and
we had to field. He was not impressed by the intellectual
qualifications of R. A. Hutton, BA (Cantab).

Around the country we had our own particular calling
spots: pubs with a notably good pint, cafés which would
throw together the most enormous grill for half-a-crown.
There we would meet, perhaps at a halfway house en route
from Middlesbrough to Dover, exchange notes on the
adventures which had so far befallen us and speculate on
whether Closey (who drove everywhere at around the speed
of light) was up a tree or down some road works or through a
hedge. In his time he accomplished all of these and more.
In those early days I had no car of my own and my father
drove me to home games at Headingley or Park Avenue or
Bramall Lane.

On the longer journeys to away matches, it was necessary
to double up with one of the other players, sharing the
driving, and to my quite unbridled delight I was in due

course taken under the motoring wing of F. S. Trueman. By now I was accepted as a first-team player – although as yet uncapped – and I joined in the conversations, the laughter and the singing like everyone else, but I didn't talk out of turn and I didn't gratuitously offer my views on controversial topics when, for instance, Close, Illingworth and Binks were holding a violent and colourful inquest on something that had gone wrong. Also, I still indulged in my private hero-worship and Fred was an heroic figure of the greatest magnitude. In my cricketing Heaven, he was God. All my life I have known that I would have gone over the top and charged the enemy trenches without a weapon in my hand if Fred had commanded. So when FST invited me to travel with him I was in seventh heaven. Now throughout the 1950s and most of the 1960s, Freddie Trueman could walk into any pub in the land, be instantly recognised and find due obeisance made. In middle age now, he keeps a careful watch on what he eats and drinks, and a gin-and-tonic is more likely to be found in his hand. But in his heyday a pint of bitter was an essential prop in the Trueman one-man extravaganza. He didn't drink many of them but they were always to hand – a symbol. Fred not only bowled fast; he *was* a fast bowler to very depths of his soul. When he was not radiating outright hostility, a smouldering belligerence lay gently flickering not too far beneath the surface. When he was dispensing bonhomie in relatively strange company there was an un-spoken warning against undue familiarity. He was an actor – an obvious one, true, but he knew his stage and he knew his audience. If anyone failed to appreciate this, God help him! When the two of us were alone in the car together he could be a marvellously stimulating companion; he had an endless string of anecdotes, most of them demolishing in one pungent phrase men whose reputations to me ensured them permanent domicile in cricket's Hall of Fame. Fred's graphic denunciations reduced them to something less than ordinary mortality. I would sit beside him hour after hour as he talked of Tests and Test cricketers, legends to me, as though he was reciting a railway timetable.

Fred at all times has loved an audience, and I was more than content that on such occasions the audience was me. He could talk superb cricket sense and he could give sage cricket advice; I lapped up both. And then, on the horizon, a red neon sign would appear proclaiming our impending arrival at a Double Diamond dispensary. 'Double Diamond, my little mate?' came the inevitable question. 'Double Diamond, Fred,' was the immediate response. We walked into the pub and the Trueman Transformation Scene took place. We were no longer two friends driving together from one match to another. Fred was now on stage. His public were the customers whose quiet contemplation of their evening pint was suddenly converted, in that instant, into participation in The Greatest Show on (Cricket's) Earth. The one and only F. S. Trueman had arrived. Fred's jacket was suddenly thrust to the back of his shoulders, the chin jutted, the pipe projected even further as he hustled to the bar. Henry Irving never made greater impact with a stage entrance than Freddie Trueman in a pub. The locals made room at the bar, then formed a respectful semi-circle. 'Evening, Mr Trueman.' 'Evening, my old flower.' Occasionally, some daring soul would venture, 'Evening, Fred,' and would immediately and comprehensively be reduced by a single glance to a pile of shivering ashes on the floor.

I was content to lurk in his shadow. 'What'll you have, Mr Trueman – a pint?' 'That's very good of you, my old flower. And my little mate here, Jake Hampshire, he'll have a pint as well.' Pint followed pint into my glass, with a modest half into Fred's after the initial symbolic rites had been observed. His pint glass at his elbow, like the royal sceptre, indicated that King Frederick was holding court. The actual stuff that works wonders went into the glass of his acolyte, standing modestly in the wings. In any pub we visited (and we visited many, over the years) they will tell you to this day of the evening when Freddie Trueman called and drank ten pints on his way to annihilate Warwickshire or Sussex or Northants, and they will genuinely believe it. Fred today hates the legend, but at the time he not only loved it, it was necessary to him; the Trueman legend had to be sustained and nurtured. And it was – at the expense, usually, of my bladder. Out we would go to the car, where Fred handed over the keys with the royal command, 'Right, my little mate, you carry on.' And with that he would crash out into untroubled slumber.

Blinking blearily through the windscreen, inching forward onto the edge of my seat, I would lurch uncertainly over the English lanes to Edgbaston or Hove or Northampton. I didn't mind too much, apart from certain physical discomforts; I would gladly have got out and pulled the car along the remainder of its trip with FS as the passenger. I loved him, respected him, admired him. He could be boastful, vain, outrageous. But when we faced the opposition next day, Fred delivered. In cricket there are always colourful personalities around, but to be a great character you first of all have to be a great player. At his peak, during those years I was privileged to be in the same team (not to mention the same car), Fred was the Greatest.

6

A Present from Charlie Griffith

On 15, 16 and 17 May 1963, Yorkshire played the West Indies at Middlesbrough and beat them. This was the West Indies of Frankie Worrell, of Sobers, of Basil Butcher, Rohan Kanhai and Wes Hall. It was the West Indies of Charlie Griffith. That game, and Charlie Griffith, affected my whole life.

We batted first and I opened with Doug Padgett. Now the light in England is inferior to the light in any other country when it comes to batting, sight-screen backing in England in the 1960s was not exactly the best in the world, and Charlie Griffith was not the most perfect of fast bowlers the game has ever seen. In the Lord's Test he and Wes Hall battered Brian Close until the whole of his right side was a mass of bruises and Closey, while respecting Hall as a great bowler, has never made any bones about his firm belief that Griffith actually threw his bouncer and his yorker. Nor has any batsman of my acquaintance who faced Charlie on that tour. So let me join the club. He came in, and to say that he bowled would be dignifying the delivery with legitimacy. He threw it. Before I had even started to pick up my bat, the ball struck me on the temple. I went down like a pole-axed bullock and I knew nothing for a few minutes. When I staggered to my feet I tottered around in agony and in a totally dazed state. If I had been a boxer the contest would have been stopped on the

38

grounds that I was no longer capable of defending myself. Then I collapsed again.

Eventually I was revived sufficiently to be helped off the field and all I can remember about that lurch back to the dressing room is seeing Philip Sharpe coming out to take my place. Now Sharpie to me has always been like the full moon coming up, with his night-club tan and round face, and I didn't blame him at all if it was a bit whiter than usual at the moment. He gave me the raised eyebrows and went on his way rejoicing, to face Charlie the Chucker. I was stretched out on the dressing room table with all the lads crowding anxiously round, and it's strange how odd, fleeting seconds of that befuddled state come back to me. Here I had a glimpse of priorities, Yorkshire cricket-style. The face of captain, D. B. Close, appeared in the gallery above me and as I opened my eyes, he very earnestly imparted this advice: 'Johnnie, if you ever get hit again, make sure you drop *inside* the crease, or they can run you out.'

At that moment, I was not entirely sure whether I was in this world or the next. I had just gone through an experience which I had never encountered, or even contemplated, in my life. If I had been able to think so far ahead, I might well have dwelt on how I was going out to face Charlie Griffith again. But maybe that was the moment when I started to come round just a little because I remember hearing my captain's advice and thinking, 'What a four-letter-word!'

But that was Closey all over. He had absolutely no sense of physical fear himself, and he ignored as irrelevant any suggestion of danger as a batsman or as a fielder; and while he didn't expect everyone to be exactly as he was, his priorities were just a little different from those of us who are subject to human frailties. We've all seen him standing at short leg or silly point with blood pouring down his leg or his face after taking a full smash and snarling at the bowler to get on with it because 'we've got to take these last three wickets'. No-one but Closey would have reasoned (reasoned?) that the way to play Hall and Griffith at Lord's was to walk down the pitch to meet the ball 'because that way they're not going to bowl me and I can't be lbw'. Dear old Closey. We all thought he was potty at times but my, how we respected him.

I was pretty groggy but we lost a lot of wickets and I had to go out and bat again in the afternoon. We then bowled West Indies out for 109, got a first-innings lead of 117 and on the second afternoon I was in action again. This time I watched as Padgett was felled; he took no further part in the game. Again, a pale-faced P. J. Sharpe had to man the barricades! At one stage of that innings I was hit on the pad by Frankie Worrell and I picked the ball up and tossed it back to the bowler. At the end of the game our chairman approached me – the redoubtable Brian Sellers, straight-talking, hard-hitting, uncompromising, autocratic, the 'Crackerjack', as he was known to his Yorkshire team of the 'thirties. 'Ah, a little official sympathy from on high,' I thought. Not so. 'Look here, young Hampshire,' he roared, 'one thing you *don't* do is pick the ———— ball up and bowl it back to the ———— bowler.' Another lesson. I've never done it since that day.

If there can be any lighter sides to a terrible blow on the head, then I suppose those are some of them. Unhappily, there were far more unpleasant repercussions for me.

From that day – 15 May 1963 – I have never had a full night's sleep. I have read enough paperbacks through the still watches of the night to fill Rotherham Public Library; I have walked the streets of the cricketing cities of England with only stray dogs for company. If I get four hours sleep in a night, twenty years later, I think I have done well, and this has inevitably affected the whole course of my life. Possibly the most frequent criticism to be levelled at my batting throughout my career is that too often I have lost my wicket when I ought to have been solidly 'in', with my score in the forties and fifties. It's a valid criticism. Certainly I have lost, or been unable to maintain, my concentration on many occasions when I have otherwise felt to be in good nick, and I can put it down every time to that crack on the head from Charlie Griffith. If I had been sent to hospital for an X-ray it might possibly have done something to prevent those after-effects which have been with me for so long. We shall never know. But I can never think of Charlie Griffith without bitterness because I am quite, quite convinced that that day marked a turning point in my life and affected the whole of my career ever afterwards. There was the coldest of cold comfort later in the evening when Rohan Kanhai said to me, 'Well, Hamp, you've one consolation. If it had happened in the West Indies, on our wickets, you would have been dead.'

In August of the same season, Yorkshire met West Indies for a second time and once again I had to open the batting against Griffith, this time reinforced by Wes Hall and Gary Sobers. I batted for a long time in each innings, and Ted Lester, our scorer, reckoned I took 80 per cent of Griffith's bowling. I never flinched and I never got out of line. And I was scared stupid the whole of the time I was batting. Boycott, at the other end, rates it one of the best efforts he has ever seen. But 15 May 1963 remains by far the most significant day's cricket in the whole of my career. Twenty years later it still affects my life as it has affected all the 7000-odd days and nights in between.

Because I did not know this trauma was going to follow me through the next two decades, there was cause for rejoicing in 1963, too; you might say that the high and low points of my life came in that season. There have not been many highs to match that at Cardiff Arms Park on the morning of Friday 26 July. Closey and Fred were away at the Headingley Test and Illy was the captain against Glamorgan. We had declared at 332 for 7 and bowled them out for 88. It was an obvious case for enforcing the follow-on but at the same time our bowlers were a bit tired in the latter part of the second day. Also, Bob Platt had broken down and we had to give him a bit of a rub-down on the field before he could get back to the dressing room. So we were a bowler short and, with the twelfth man acting as emergency fieldsman, we were also short of someone to organise the teas and the close-of-play drinks. We pressed into service one of the press corps (a Yorkshire-born reporter, of course!) who, not entirely by coincidence, was to become my collaborator in this book 20 years later.

As the afternoon wore on, and Glamorgan were proving rather more difficult to dislodge than they had been in the morning, I decided on a little diversion by calling for a cap I didn't need. Our dressing room twelfth man, sensing what was afoot but being unable to ignore the summons, found my cap and, as Don Wilson was about to start an over, set off along the corridor which in those days separated the high temple of Welsh rugby from the cricket ground which is now Cardiff's club pitch. His reasoning was that one ball would be delivered while he was out of sight of play, so that when he reached the gates he counted five more deliveries from Wilson before trotting out onto the field bearing my cap. What he didn't know was that the start of the over had been delayed while he was in the corridor and he was now on his way out to the middle after only five balls. The umpire, Paul Gibb, shooed him away, clucking his indignation, whereupon the northern cricket correspondent of the *Daily Mail*, not entirely inconspicuous in a bright red shirt, snarled that Paul had never been able to count and it was in fact the end of the over. This caused Don Wilson, as he waited to deliver the final ball, to collapse with laughter and the whole team joined in. One furious cricket writer hurled down the cap, stormed off the field and was met at the gates by an equally furious Wilf Wooller, the High Priest of the Temple, who was apoplectic at the invasion of *his* cricket field by a gaudily garbed trespasser. During the tea interval there were harsh recriminations on one side and hysterical laughter on the other – one sheepish scribe and eleven convulsed cricketers. Happily, our friendship has survived the incident and the passing years.

On the first day of the match I had become the first batsman to put a ball through the windows of the Cardiff Athletic Club at long-on. In the Glamorgan second innings I had run out Bernard Hedges with a long throw, as he went for a third run. These adventures, plus the cap incident, naturally enough focussed the captain's attention upon me to some extent, but maybe it was just a stroke of Illingworth intuition which prompted him to give me the ball. My leg-spinning youth was now lost in the mists of time but I had bowled a lot in the nets and it was known that I could do a bit of leg-spinning. I was delighted to have a go and I have never forgotten the glee of dismissing little Alan Rees with the help of a slip catch by Dick Hutton. I bet Rees hasn't, either. Up to that point I had bowled just nine overs in Championship cricket without taking a wicket and it is never pleasant to be the first victim. He was a super chap, Alan Rees, and we had a laugh or two about it in later years, but it can't have been much of a joke for him at the time. I got one more wicket before close of play but I was still surprised when Illy told me that evening, 'I'm going to start with you in the morning.' It didn't seem logical if there was some turn, when Illy himself and Don Wilson were available, but I certainly wasn't going to argue about it. By 11.45 it was all over. We had won by an innings and 66 runs and for evermore the reference books were going to have to record that J. H. Hampshire, RHB, was now also LBG with a BB of 13–2–52–7 v. Glam (Cardiff) 26/7/63.

I was as tickled as a kid with a new toy as we drove up to Worcester for the next game. It was a different story there, on the flattest of flat wickets (come to think of it, that hasn't

changed much) and Don Kenyon, Tom Graveney and Dick
Richardson hammering it all over the place. For some reason
which now escapes me, Wilson and I decided on a policy of
'they shall not pass' and we put on what Illy described as the
greatest sustained piece of outfielding he had ever seen. He
reckoned we saved between 80 or 100 runs in the field but we
still lost by an innings and drove up to Scarborough in a
chastened mood. However, things looked up in the remaining half-dozen games and after beating Leicestershire in two
consecutive matches, the last two of the season, we finished
as champions in my first full season in senior cricket,
with two wins and 20 points more than the runners-up –
Glamorgan! In the circumstances I suppose I might have
reflected that a performance of 7 for 52 in Cardiff was worth
double its face value.

In October I went into hospital where deep X-rays showed
there was still internal bruising as a legacy from C. Griffith,
five months earlier. I had not had a night's sleep throughout the season. I still experienced excruciating pains. My
physical confidence might have been impaired but my
psychological fears had been enhanced. But in a strange,
mixed-up way I had at the same time loved so much of my
summer. I had played a full season for Yorkshire; I had
played my cricket with Freddie Trueman and Brian Close
and Ray Illingworth and was part of the same team as these
great figures. If the belt from Charlie Griffith gave me night-
mares, there were a lot of pleasant dreams which had come
true. And in October I read in the *Yorkshire Post* that
Yorkshire CCC had awarded county caps to G. Boycott,
J. H. Hampshire and A. G. Nicholson.

7
'Dear John'

My winters were still being spent in the printing works where I had to 'clock on' at 7.45 in the morning, so I collected the morning papers before catching the bus. That is how I learned I had been 'capped' by Yorkshire on 2 October 1963. There was no formal intimation to me at home, just the bald announcement that the three of us – Boycott, Nicholson and Hampshire – were now fully fledged Yorkshire players. It was the most marvellous feeling. Another dream had been realised and, as mercenary considerations mixed with more romantic reactions, I mused that I was now paid the same salary as Close, Trueman and Illingworth. That was utterly incredible, quite unbelievable. Still I had not achieved a complete belief in my own ability and at the same time the past season had served to enhance my respect and admiration for Yorkshire's senior players to an even greater degree. Closey, Fred and Illy were what cricket was all about as far as I was concerned. As I played alongside them, I still hero-worshipped all of them, just as I came to have that same star-struck admiration for Ian Botham twenty years later. I suppose it was just the way I am made – an attitude perhaps induced by my childhood reading of those wonderful D. C. Thomson publications, the *Hotspur* and *Wizard* and *Rover*. They created heroes for the childish imagination and my adult life had led me into a world where such figures were real: not merely as large as life but sometimes very much larger! Brian Close, in his own autobiography, recalls his

45

wonderment at the moment when he realised he was now paid the same money as Len Hutton. Now, I had joined him in my turn in the salary scale.

I reached the printing works that morning in a state of bemused delight. Something had to be done to recognise my new status and, indeed, my recently-acquired affluence, because Yorkshire have always tried to pay their players well. I was certainly now on good money so I ordered a cup of tea for everyone, all round the works – it cost me about three quid at a penny a cup! In due course a Yorkshire player's tie arrived through the post, and I looked at it lovingly. That white dog-rose with 12 petals has always been the subject of a certain amount of ribaldry within the Yorkshire ranks, but God help anyone else who criticised it. It hasn't the horticultural attractiveness of Lancashire's red rose or the heraldic precision of the Tudor rose of Northants, Derbyshire or Hampshire, but the Yorkshire rose, on cap, blazer or tie, is just about the most precious symbol ever to come into the possession of a cricketer – or it used to be, at any rate.

With my tie came a letter from the secretary, John Nash, confirming my 'cap' and addressing me for the first time as 'Dear John'. All previous communications had curtly begun 'Dear Hampshire', and the significance of this was not lost on me. Now I had really arrived. I used to resent the patronising use of my surname in a peculiarly Yorkshire fashion. In a number of different walks of life, Yorkshiremen are quite feudal while at the same time harbouring a bitter resentment of feudalism. Fred Trueman used to fume with rage when Brian Sellers addressed him simply by his surname and the 'Crackerjack' was marvellously anachronistic in this. He was the Great Democrat, the man who called spades bloody shovels. He would curse and swear and treat the opposition like mortal enemies. His language was that of a navvy to his work-mate, labouring on a building site, but his attitude was that of the CO to the humblest private. It is the sort of social contradiction which may not be unique to Yorkshire but is certainly found there more than anywhere else, and the resentment matches the attitude itself. My first reaction on being addressed as 'Hampshire' had been to reply 'Dear Nash' but mercifully, in those early days I used to show all my letters to my father for a final check on spelling and grammar. Neither of these considerations excited his attention as his eyes focused on the form of address. 'You can't send that,' he declared with some emphasis. 'Do it again, starting "Dear *Mr* Nash".'

So here I was, at last being addressed as an adult with some standing in the community, and I had that tattered dog-daisy on my tie. I am not known as an emotional bloke but I looked at it with loving eyes and with feelings that I find difficult to express. I wore it with great pride for the next twenty years. The cap, however, did not arrive that winter and, remembering how my father's 2nd XI cap had been an object of reverence in the Hampshire household, I suppose it is not difficult to appreciate the impatience with which I waited for that. It was not until we reported for pre-season training in 1964 that I was to lay hands on it and then it was in circumstances of overwhelming anti-climax. Such was the significance of a Yorkshire cap, so earnestly had I looked forward to winning mine, that I had built up in my mind a vision of a presentation ceremony of some solemnity. Generally when new caps are awarded, they are presented in the course of a game in which the newly capped player is involved, and even if it is handed over in the dressing room or the luncheon room, there is a certain dignity and sense of occasion. To my intense disappointment, nothing like that was in store for me. Before the first training session I went to the Yorkshire headquarters, then housed in the city centre of Leeds. I was feeling pretty chuffed; it was a big moment in my life, even if it was six months after the announcement, and I was still on cloud nine. Miss Coates, John Nash's secretary, was there and I told her, 'I've come for my cap, Miss Coates.' She walked to the back of the office, came back with a brown cardboard box and said, 'There you are. Help yourself.' I was utterly deflated. I don't think I had ever worn a cap up to that point (except that day at Cardiff) and in the years which followed I rarely wore one, but that was not the point. Simply getting that cap meant more to me than any England cap in the future was ever to mean, and to have to rummage around in a box full of caps until I found one to fit me seemed the most demoralising experience possible. I went round to Billy Sutcliffe's sports goods shop, picked up my county sweaters and carried on to Headingley fully equipped as a first-team player for the first training session of 1964. But somehow a little of the magic had gone out of my life.

Despite the lack of ceremony, I had moved another rung up the ladder. There were about 20 more to climb, I estimated. In June, we played Bobbie Simpson's Australians at Bramall Lane and the South Yorkshire cricketing public turned up in force. Judy and I had decided to get married at the end of the year and she was there to see me play, along with most of my family. I was really keyed up, remembering the hundred I had scored against the '61 Aussies for Minor Counties. It all meant so much to me. Probably it meant too much because I was out without scoring and it plunged me into the depths of darkest despair. The Australians had declared towards the end of the first day and I was caught behind off the finest brush against a glove.

I have never felt so completely dismayed in my life. I dashed away from the ground, went into the front room at home and sobbed my heart out, such was the crushing feeling of disappointment. Judy had to find her way home on the bus and when my parents got back they found me in bed, sick to the depths of my soul. My father tried to talk to me, to make me feel just a little less despairing, but it was no good. If I had looked at him I would have burst into tears all over again.

That was what it meant to play for Yorkshire and to fail. My cricketing insecurity was rearing its menacing head once again. I so desperately wanted to succeed that batting failure became an overwhelming personal tragedy. That Saturday evening I felt that my whole damned life had been shot to pieces.

The second game against the tourists was at Bradford and I had my first experience of the sardonic humour which was a speciality of the Park Avenue crowds. Every Yorkshire ground has its own atmosphere and its spectators have their own characteristics. There is a special dourness about the Bradford contingent, perhaps because for so many years the wicket there was a seam-bowler's dream and spectators became used to seeing batsmen who had to work hard for every run. It was that way in the early 'sixties but I struck the ball pretty well and got 42 runs in quick time. As I went back to the pavilion, bowled Hawke, I felt I had done my bit towards the entertainment value of the day, only to hear a disgruntled Bradford voice enquire, 'What's tha think this is – t'bloody Scarborough Festival, or what?' Not easy to satsify, the Park Avenue multitude. Don Wilson once took five for very few there and got a good write-up in the papers for it. The following day, the author of one of those laudatory pieces was strolling round the ground when he was stopped by two of the sages who always occupied the same splintered bench on the Horton Park side of the ground. 'It's all reight tha going on abaht that Wilson feller,' they complained, 'but tha's got to remember that we were browt up on Wilfred Rhodes and George Herbert Hirst. Na they were *real* bawlers.'

'But surely they had good days and bad days like everybody else?' asked the pressman, defensively.

They gazed at him in stark disbelief. 'Bad days?' they chorused. 'Bad days? Rhodes and Hirst? NIVVER.' And they turned away from the Philistine who had uttered the heresy.

In that Bradford game, Boycott got a hundred against the Aussies in the face of some awful stick from them. The great Australian hate-hate relationship with Boycott had begun as early as that, and when you think of the runs he has taken off their bowling over the years, always in an atmosphere of naked hostility, you really have to take your hat off to him. He has been a target for criticism, for bumper attacks, for general hostility all his cricketing life, and out in the middle he has generally contrived to say nowt and get on with the job. You have got to give him full credit for that. It was Derek Underwood who, when Boycs came home from India in the middle of the 1981–82 tour, voiced the old pro's view of Geoffrey Boycott: 'There are a lot of knockers around when Boycs is talked about, but anyone who has seen him out in the middle, battling it out against the most hostile of bowling for hour after hour, will always respect that side of him.' His answer to the Aussies was to make his first Test century against them at the Oval. He has never been their favourite opponent.

The fifth Test was a notable one for Yorkshire cricket because apart from Boycott's maiden hundred, it also produced Fred Trueman's three hundredth Test wicket – the famous dismissal of Neil Hawke. Yorkshire completed a game at Hove on the day that the Test finished and our pair of heroes rejoined us for the next Championship match at Dover. There had been quite a bit of champagne left over from the celebrations at the Oval and a couple of Yorkshiremen were never going to let that be wasted, so a fair supply of bubbly found its way to Dover in Fred's car. With it came the biggest pile of congratulatory letters and telegrams anyone has ever seen. They just about filled the back of Fred's Jaguar, and I spent most of the day opening and sorting them for him. That Kent game is memorable for Ray Illingworth's performance; he scored 135 out of our total of 256, which was enough to give us a win by an innings and 11 runs as Illy followed up his ton by taking 14 wickets for 101 (7 for 49 and 7 for 52) – an incredible performance. Not surprisingly, Dover remains Illy's favourite ground to this day.

So one way and another we had quite a bit to celebrate, and with the help of Fred's champers and the co-operation of a genial manager of the White Cliffs Hotel, we celebrated to some tune. Late at night a determined body of Yorkshiremen descended from the esplanade to the beach to embark upon a massed-start Channel swim. It was not until the water rose to lap around the more delicate parts of the anatomy that feeling – and with it commonsense – penetrated the anaesthetising properties of the drink. It was a rather hung-over party which made its way to the Oval for the next match against Surrey. There was to be no Championship that year. Worcestershire 'walked it' with 18 wins, four more than any-one else but we had added another Yorkshire name to the list of those who had hit Test centuries (and against the Aussies, too) and the one and only FST had achieved immortality by becoming the first bowler ever to take 300 Test wickets. We would have liked the Championship too, of course, and there would be those up north who would be witch-hunting be-cause we had not taken it once again. But under the heady influence of last night's champagne the cricket world didn't seem a bad old place on the morning of 22 August 1964 – even with a splitting headache!

8

Tasmania

1965 was the year which saw Yorkshire win the Gillette Cup in some style and it also marked a significant change in my way of life. The Gillette Final, at Lord's on 4 September, saw us total 317 for 4 after being put in by Surrey. We were home and dry by the time our innings had ended: no team of our corporate ability and all-round experience was going to allow the opposition to score 318 in the second innings of a one-day match, and we eventually won by a massive 175 runs. But it might never have happened. We got off to a rather slow start and there were some restive stirrings on our dressing room balcony as Boycott and Ken Taylor reached only 22 with the overs seeming to shoot by. A conference by our general staff decided on a change in the batting order when the first wicket fell, and instead of Duggie Padgett going in at no. 3, Closey took over. The reasoning behind this was that (a) the left-hand batsman would be better able to counter Dave Sydenham's left-arm over the wicket attack, which was proving disturbingly economical, and (b) our commander-in-chief could direct things better out in the middle. Close has since said that he gave Geoff Boycott the hard word about getting on with it, and he himself proceeded to play a beautiful cameo of an innings of 79 so that from 22 for 1 we reached 214 for 2 when the captain was out. He either inspired or frightened Boycott into playing arguably the greatest innings of his life. His 146 was masterly, to say the least, and we were able to mount a late-innings thrash

without calling upon the batting of Padgett, Sharpe, Illingworth or Hutton.

During that season, in fact during the Roses match at Old
Trafford, a letter had passed around the dressing room asking if anyone was interested in a coaching appointment in
Tasmania during our winter. It would be a three-year contract and I was very interested indeed. I had completed my
apprenticeship in printing and had been working for the
Rotherham Advertiser as a representative, but after being
capped by Yorkshire, my cricket was now the major factor in
my working life. At the same time I was getting a hint or two
from my winter employers that I would very shortly have to
decide between cricket and printing as my major occupation.
There was no doubt in my mind that cricket would take
precedence, but there remained the problem of finding
something to do to earn a living outside the cricket season.

Coaching in the sunshine of the Australian continent
seemed a pleasant solution to the problem, especially as the
post carried that three-year contract. We were shortly to
experience in Yorkshire the first rumblings of discontent
with a system which meant we were simply employed from
one season to the next under a gentleman's agreement. There
was no security beyond that one season, no long-term future
to be faced with confidence and peace of mind. It was Ray
Illingworth's attempt to change this, and his failure to get
any response out of a county committee which had seen the
system work throughout the whole history of the club and
saw no reason to change it, that led to his leaving Yorkshire
for Leicestershire. That move led to the birth of Leicestershire as a real cricketing power, just as Close's move to
Somerset two years later was to create a similar miracle there
while Yorkshire, unbelievably, slumped to a second-rate
(and sometimes, it seemed, a third-rate) power in the game.

But no-one, least of all me, even dreamed of such disasters
in the summer of 1965. Illingworth was enjoying a benefit

season and the club's annual report, while expressing disappointment at only finishing fourth in the County Championship, referred to the club's 'year of triumph' in the Gillette and thanked Mr D. B. Close for his 'invaluable services' as first-team captain. The storm clouds had not yet started to gather, even on the distant horizon. I was happy in the only security a Yorkshire cricketer was ever likely to know (I had my cap) and my only problem was what to do with my winters. Tasmania would be the solution to that problem. I had an advanced coaching certificate and had spent part of my winters coaching at Lilleshall, so I seemed well qualified and I applied for the job. Some weeks later I saw Donald Carr at Lord's and was told that, subject to final agreement from Tasmania, the job was mine. That agreement duly arrived and I was contracted to coach there in the winters of 1966–67, 1967–68 and 1968–69. Up to that point I had had a social tour of the United States with Yorkshire and a little dabble in the West Indies with the International Cavaliers. I had never been on an MCC tour and, except in an organised party, I had never travelled abroad at all. So there we were, Judy accompanying me for a whole winter abroad, with no real idea of what it was like to travel to the other side of the world.

We set off on the Great Adventure, feeling as pleased as Punch with ourselves and dressed up to the nines in our best clothes as we flew from Leeds and Bradford airport at Yeadon, down to Heathrow to transfer to the big bird which was to fly us to Australia. The first stop was at Rome and I think there were nine others as we winged our way across the globe in a plane packed with emigrants to the sunshine of Australia in summer. At five o'clock one morning we finally staggered out of the aircraft in rain-lashed Sydney, our best clothes now fit only for a jumble sale! We wondered just what the hell we had let ourselves in for. The Customs and Immigration formalities seemed to take hours and we were more

Arthur 'Ticker' Mitchell, joint county coach when I was first invited to the Headingley nets. A dour batsman in the 1920s and 1930s, as coach he was at pains to preserve the traditional Yorkshire values. (*Yorkshire Post*)

2 Maurice Leyland, who was Arthur Mitchell's coaching colleague and temperamentally his complete opposite, giving some tips to a youthful Doug Padgett. Doug himself is now the county coach. (*Yorkshire Post*)

3 Ken Taylor cover-drives. With the pads off, he was one of the finest fielders I have ever seen. (*Central Press*)

4 The great-hearted Tony Nicholson, the best bowler of his time not to play for his country. (*Yorkshire Post*)

5 Brian Close and Fred Trueman in the early 1960s. (*Yorkshire Post*)

6 If your image in your early days involved a pint of beer as an essential prop, then I suppose there's no greater compliment than having a pub named after you! (*Ken Kelly*)

7 The Huttons, father and son. (*Yorkshire Post*)

8 Philip 'Toby Jug' Sharpe takes one of his 617 catches, this one for England against West Indies in 1969. (*Central Press*)

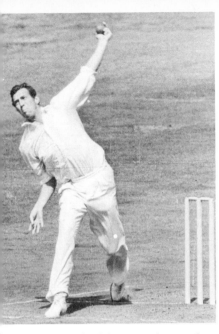

Don Wilson, a fine left-armer and a more than useful fielder. (*Sport & General*)

10 A youthful Raymond Illingworth at cold and muddy pre-season nets at Headingley. (*Yorkshire Post*)

11 Geoff Cope – more sinned against than sinning? (*Yorkshire Post*)

12 No injury problems today! All fire and energy, Chris Old lets go another thunderbolt. (*Bob Thomas*)

13   Yorkshire in 1964. *Standing:*
Phil Sharpe, Don Wilson, John
Waring, John Hampshire, Geoffrey
Boycott, Doug Padgett. *Seated:*
Jimmy Binks, Fred Trueman,
Brian Close, Ray Illingworth,
Ken Taylor.

14   Brian Sellers, the Yorkshire
CCC chairman whose autocratic
rejection of Ray Illingworth's
request for a contract in 1967
sowed the seeds of the club's
difficulties over the next 15 years.
(*Yorkshire Post*)

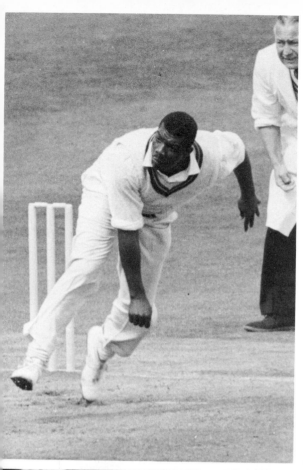

15 & 16   You meet all sorts of people in cricket! The hostility and aggression of my particular bugbear, Charlie Griffith (*left*), contrast with the charm and grace of HRH the Duchess of Kent, the Patron of Yorkshire CCC (*below*). On my right is my wife, Judy, and in the background a youthful Chris Old and his wife.   (*Sport & General/Sheffield Newspapers Ltd*)

17 Congratulations from Gary Sobers on my century in my first Test – Lord's, 28 June 1969. Mike Findlay watches, Steve Camacho in the foreground. (*Sport & General*)

18 The England team for the third Test against the West Indies at Headingley in 1969. *Standing:* Phil Sharpe, John Snow, David Brown, Derek Underwood, Basil d'Oliveira, John Hampshire. *Seated:* Barry Knight, Geoffrey Boycott, Ray Illingworth, John Edrich, Alan Knott. (*Central Press*)

19 *Left:* Geoffrey Boycott at his most eloquent, with a bat in his hands. (*George Herringshaw*)

20 *Below:* One of the other sides of Geoffrey Boycott – pressurised by the media. (*Jack Hickes*)

21　Yorkshire in 1979. *Back row:* Howard Cooper, Kevin Sharp, Jim Love, Bill Athey. *Middle row:* Graham Stevenson, Phil Carrick, Arnie Sidebottom, Richard Lumb, Peter Whiteley, Colin Johnson. *Front row:* David Bairstow, Geoffrey Boycott, John Hampshire, Ray Illingworth, Chris Old, Geoff Cope.

22　For me, the last straw was Scarborough on 9 September 1981. A solitary spectator applauds as Richard Lumb and Martin Moxon go out to open the Yorkshire innings from a pavilion of glum faces and amid a buzz of speculation. (*Dennis Dobson*)

dead than alive when we eventually got through them all. By the time we flew into Hobart at five o'clock that afternoon, we were more completely shattered than we had ever felt in our lives and already slightly disillusioned with the glamour of world travel. There was a reception by a large crowd of cricket officials and supporters at the airport, and I then discovered that there had been no coach there since the 1920s when they had had another Yorkshire player by the name of Hughie Myers. So it was something of a VIP reception and I was whisked off to TV and radio studios.

We had arrived in the Australian spring and everywhere was a mass of apple blossom so that it seemed as if there had been a heavy snowfall. It's a beautiful island and until a suitable flat was found for us we were accommodated at a little pub in a place called Sandy Bay. The University was my coaching headquarters, and I made friendships there which still continue today. Socially, our life was very pleasant and I was doing quite well playing in district cricket. But the structure of coaching was very shaky indeed and it all had to be built up from scratch. Its deficiencies were by no means the result of lack of effort, but there had been no organised administration for so long that it seemed to me that dozens of well-meaning people were rushing around in circles and getting nowhere fast.

Administration has never been my strong point, and I expect I was pretty outspoken when I looked around their set-up, so the Tasmanians can't have been very impressed at having a Pom tell them what was what. All in all, I was just about ready to come home at Christmas, but then a couple of things happened. First, it snowed on Mount Nelson on Christmas Eve, which is of course midsummer in Tasmania! We had a good Christmas party at the pub where we had stayed during our first weeks in the island and life began to seem a little less frustrating. From snow on Christmas Eve, we had an air temperature of 101 degrees on Christmas Day, and from that moment we never saw another cloud in the sky. The heat built up and a combination of tinder-dry undergrowth and a bit of carelessness up in the country produced the worst bush-fire in Australian history. On 7 February it was as if the whole of southern Tasmania suddenly exploded. 70 people were killed in one day; livestock were burned to cinders; homes were razed by the score. For a time it was wholesale carnage.

I had no coaching sessions fixed for that day and Judy, who had got herself a secretarial job in the city, had been home at lunchtime and we had had a swim to try to keep cool. She went back to work and by 2.30 in the afternoon it was clear that something very unpleasant indeed was happening. The temperature built up even higher; there was so much smoke in the air that you couldn't see a hand in front of you; the heat was so intense that the brewery blew up, the metalwork of buses buckled, anything made of plastic simply melted away and brick-built houses exploded. I set off into town to look for Judy and spent about four hours searching; in the meantime, she had been driven home and was wondering where I was. Eventually we met up at our flat which was at the foot of Mount Nelson. Halfway up the mountain lived a friend of ours, Bob Cotgrove, who at the time was away in Launceston which meant that his wife and baby were on their own, somewhere in the path of a raging bushfire. Peter Hadlow, the secretary of the Tasmanian Cricket Association, helped me fill up my old banger of a car with wet sacks and off we went up the hill. For anyone who has never seen a bush-fire it will be difficult to picture the scene, but try to imagine great groves of gum-trees with the fire racing through the upper branches, streaking across the countryside. As the branches split and burst, the burning gum drops to the ground, setting alight anything in its path. The whole scene was like something out of Dante's *Inferno*.

We found, thank God, that the fire had 'jumped' our

friend's house by the sort of miracle that sometimes happens, and with the homes on both sides blazing furiously, mother and baby were sitting, terrified, wondering just how to get to safety. With the help of the sacks we got them both into the car, but by now it was so hot that we simply could not breathe with the windows closed so we had to lurch back down the hillside with smoke choking us and sparks flying into and around the car. Thank the Lord for those wet sacks! Gloria Cotgrove and infant were parked in our flat and then we saw the fire begin to creep down the mountainside towards us. We were pretty vulnerable, living on the edge of a stretch of parkland with its share of gum-trees, but in the other direction, 300 yards away, was the sea. So I turned the car to face the sea, telling Judy, 'If the worst comes to the worst we're going to drive down there and straight into the water.' But first we tried a bit of self-help by chopping down the trees nearest to the back of our place to create a fire-break. Gradually the winds dropped from something like gale-force, and the fire never reached us, but it did reach a lot of other people on Black Tuesday, 7 February 1967.

By this time I had more or less come to terms with the tangled coaching set-up and I realised that there was nothing to do but try to get it sorted out. My first year as Tasmanian Cricket Association coach was not going to be an unqualified success but we would now have something to build on in the next two years of my contract. In the meantime Alex Bannister, cricket correspondent of the *Daily Mail*, had written inviting me to join an international touring side in Pakistan under Richie Benaud's captaincy and while Judy flew home to our spring, I spent four or five weeks on tour. There I had my first introduction to dysentery and I shall be more than grateful if I never have another, but I was seeing a bit of the world all at once.

My second year in Tasmania went much more smoothly, largely because we had drawn up detailed plans for a coaching system before I ended my first season there. Consequently I was able to plunge straight into a routine which meant pretty hard work, leaving home at 8.30 am and getting home just about 12 hours later, but being closely associated with the University was a tremendous help. We were a young couple surrounded by young people, and it suited us fine when we could entertain at week-ends. We did quite a lot of this as word got round that Judy was rather useful at making Yorkshire pudding! I was quite successful in grade cricket and hit 80 in Hobart and a hundred in Launceston against the touring Indians. I managed to persuade quite a few cricket authorities to lay down concrete-based wickets over which we stretched scrim matting, a kind of fine sackcloth which gave a uniform bounce and allowed the ball to come onto the bat. It was ideal for practice and so for coaching. We were making progress.

My winters in Tasmania were giving me a greater self-confidence. The island may not be part of the Australian mainland but its inhabitants are most certainly Australians and anyone not prepared to give as good as he got in verbal exchanges was doomed. I might have been invited out there in the first place, but I was still a Pom telling Aussies how to play cricket. Oh yes – my self-confidence developed. My cricket improved, too, and we both liked the life-style so it was all very different from those first three months when I was on the verge of despair. For my third term, however, a different sort of problem had arisen: our first son, Ian, was on the way. After discussing the whole matter over and over again we decided that Judy would stay at home for the birth because she wanted to be near her own mother, and I would go to Tasmania alone to honour my contract. Barbara Adams, who was the Matron at Christ College, had a spare room which the University allowed her to let to me, and she looked after me like a mother.

It was a momentous time all round, because the West

Indies were touring and although Wes and Charlie might have been past their peak, they could still let one or two go when they felt like it. Up to that time Len Maddocks had skippered the State side but in 1969 I was given the captaincy. I had no say in the choice of the side, which was carried out by the selectors. I had always felt that Tasmanian sides scarcely represented the best of the material which was available because the southern area was dominated by Hobart, the north by Launceston and the north-east by Devonport, and while numerically-based representation of those areas kept a political balance, it didn't always provide the best team. Anyway, that wasn't my problem; I simply had to run things on the field. In the meantime a phone call from England had announced that I was now the father of a son, which took about three days out of that particular week, and I celebrated with 120 against the touring side with Wes Hall leading the attack. My old friend, C. Griffith, saved himself for the second game at Launceston. I remembered him well. . . .

There had never been any love lost between us since that day in Middlesbrough and we both knew it. At Launceston I played a couple of balls and then he let me have the short one. I had been expecting it and I flung my bat and hit him out of the ground for six. Back he went, clearly displeased, and came steaming in to bowl one which didn't quite get up. I hit it through the covers for four, and followed it with one over cover for another four. That over gave me a lot of satisfaction and made up for some of the insomnia I had suffered during the previous six years. It helped a bit that the other Windies players, who clearly knew very well what it was all about, were now laughing at Charlie. I felt I had won that round. I went on to reach 98 when Basil Butcher bowled one of his flat leg-breaks which went right through everything and I was out, b Butcher, 98. I felt that in some ways that scoreline just about summed up my career!

9

The Crown and Lions

Back in England, the Roses match of 1969 was almost a complete wash-out, but after it the Yorkshire chairman, Brian Sellers, remarked to me with elaborate casualness, 'You'd better have a word with Sutcliffe at t'week-end. He might have some news for you.' Billy Sutcliffe, son of the great Herbert, himself a former Yorkshire captain, was now an England selector. There was no real need to get wildly excited at a possibility which had been so obliquely indicated, but I telephoned Bill Sutcliffe to be told that I was in the 12 for the first Test against the West Indies at Old Trafford. Once again I experienced that conflict of emotions: I wanted to play because I badly wanted to be a Test cricketer; I didn't want to play in case I failed. I wonder how many players have felt like that on being selected? More, I suspect, than those who have said to themselves, 'Great. I know I can do it. Here's my chance to show the world.'

So on 11 June, off I went to the nets at Old Trafford, where there were a fair number of my personal supporters all asking, 'Will you be in the side?' All I could reply was, 'I don't know', because there was no indication from anyone who would be the man omitted. There was a get-together over tea and cakes for the whole party and still nothing was said, not even from the new England captain – my old team-mate, Ray Illingworth, now with Leicestershire. So I knew I was in for a more than usually sleepless night at the England team's hotel at Lymm, out in Cheshire. Sure enough, around

3 am I gave up my fight to find sleep and set out on one of those lonely nocturnal vigils in the streets of Lymm. Well, at least I hadn't done it there before. I walked round and round, my mind full of hopes and ambitions, equally full of doubts and fears. I watched dawn break over the Cheshire plain, grabbed the morning newspapers before any could be delivered to the rooms of the hotel and devoured every word of prognostication about the likely shape of the England side. Jim Swanton, the High Priest of cricket journalism, thought I would be in the side, and that was Holy Writ. I was going to be an England player at last.

Back at Old Trafford, there were more nets but still no word from the captain or selectors. The Lancashire players, who were without a match, joined in the nets and little Harry Pilling said, 'Come on, Hamp. Are you playing or not?' 'Don't know' was all I could reply, reluctant even to consider the possibility, although the High Priest had delivered his judgment. We were into the final hour before play began as I walked back to the pavilion and it was then that Ray Illingworth, ahead of me on the stairs, leaned over the balustrade to tell me, 'Sorry, Hamp. You'll be twelfth man.'

'Oh, shit,' I thought. Then, 'Great.' That was my instinctive, schizophrenic reaction to the news for which I had waited all night long. Damn it to hell – I wasn't an England player yet. Superb – there was no way I could be found wanting in this Test. And though I had been backing it each way in my mind, I now had to adjust my thinking completely.

'Twelfth' is a lonely and humble role when, two minutes earlier, you have been fancying yourself as a Test player and now you find yourself as the dressing room errand-boy. There are players who understand and make it as easy as possible for the one who has been omitted from the 12; there are others who can give him a hard time. I had a few of both categories in that dressing room. And there is more to being twelfth man than simply taking out caps and sweaters. You have to find out what each player wants for lunch since many of them prefer to stay in the dressing room rather than walk to the dining room for a formal sit-down. It's all part of keeping themselves steeped in the atmosphere of the game. There are the end-of-the-day drinks to work out and a list to prepare to give to the host county's dressing room attendant. So you have plenty of duties to occupy your mind for the first half-hour or so, which help shut out the disappointment/ exultation you feel at your non-selection. It is not long before the disappointment takes over because there is no longer any need to feel apprehension about how you would have performed had you been selected. That has now gone by the board so you can indulge yourself to the full in a sense of crushing depression. You are now the one whose talents are surplus to requirements out on the field. You permit yourself a little analysis of the side: why is So-and-so playing and not me? Suddenly, from having doubts about your right to be there, about your ability to compete at the very highest level, you now have no doubts at all about your ability and credentials. You question the wisdom of including Barry Knight (the man E. W. Swanton himself had felt might be omitted) instead of you on what looks a very useful batting pitch. But then the game begins and you force yourself to accept the situation and get on with the menial chores.

It occurred to me that I had never even seen a Test match since my grandmother had taken me to Headingley as an 11-year-old, to see Fred Trueman reduce India to 0 for 4. Had I dreamed then of stepping out onto the field as someone involved, however modestly, with the game? When I actually did so, it was in rather bizarre circumstances because Tom Graveney, batting at no. 4, had gone out to bat without a box! It took him about an over to realise that he was not only improperly but impractically dressed, because although the formidable Wes and Charlie were not on parade, Gary Sobers bowling quick could be very, very quick, and the up-and-coming Vanburn Holder was not a medium-pacer either by any means. So Tom signalled to the dressing room – a signal which, from the batsman at any rate, is not exactly well-known in cricket field semaphore and when we had finally realised what had happened, I tucked that rather vital piece of protective gear discreetly into the pocket of my flannels and trotted out to the middle where the umpires helped form a screen of modesty as Tom adjusted his dress. At last I had stepped onto a Test ground as a Test player, albeit a box-bearing twelfth man!

Ten days later I went to Lord's to join the England party for the second Test. The first had been won handsomely by ten wickets so obviously I could not expect anything other than twelfth man duties again. Or could I? Graveney was out of the party, Colin Milburn had lost an eye in that tragic road accident, Colin Cowdrey had strained his Achilles tendon, so the selectors might feel the need to bolster the batting, might they not? The wicket looked full of runs, so perhaps they would feel it better to play safe in this one, with a 1–0 lead in the series already. Or would they? The usual doubts, the inevitable hopes, all filtered through my mind during the nets, over the tea and cakes, through the weary hours until it was time to go to bed and then through the even wearier hours that stretched ahead through the night. By 3 am I was once again on the dawn patrol, this time through the streets of Maida Vale, not unnaturally attracting the attention of a young lady who seemed to be returning home after a poor night's business and sensed a possible last-minute improvement in trade. Alas for her – she could not have found a less interested potential client in the whole of London! She went on her way, muttering darkly, and I went back to the hotel, my mind a cauldron of mixed-up thoughts and aspirations.

Once again I read the morning papers before anyone else had stirred, once again I ate an early breakfast and walked, alone, to the nets across the bustling traffic of Edgware Road and along St John's Wood Road, keeping to the opposite side of the road until the very last minute lest anyone should recognise me and ask the question over which I had been agonising all night long. Sure enough, the early arrivals at the Grace Gates included a sprinkling of Yorkshiremen and the shouts began as I crossed the road. 'Morning, John. Will you play in this one?' I didn't know. I changed and walked across to the nets, and this time it was the off-duty Middlesex players who asked the question. I still didn't know. There was only an hour to go before the start of play as I walked slowly back across the most famous cricket ground in the world, torn by doubts, fired by unfulfilled ambitions. What right had I to be there? I wasn't good enough. And yet I so desperately wanted to play for England. Halfway across the ground I encountered a man who knew he was going to play, come what may. He looked up and said, 'Congratulations, Hamp. You're in.' Geoffrey Boycott was the man who told me for the first time that I was to play for England.

Now in a greater turmoil than ever, I carried on to the pavilion, not daring to seem to hurry yet wanting to get there in a split second. It couldn't be true. And yet it must be. Boycott wouldn't joke about a thing like that. As he had spoken to me, my mind had framed the words I had muttered to myself at Old Trafford, but this time their order was reversed: 'Great! Oh, shit!'

Illy looked up as I reached the dressing room: 'Well done, Hamp. You're playing. Your sweaters are in the corner. You get your cap upstairs.' I was an England Test player.

We fielded first but although it was a bit chilly I went out without my brand-new England sweater. It didn't seem right to wear it. Who was I to be walking about with the crown and lions on my chest? John Harry Hampshire from Thurnscoe was out of his depth. I wasn't good enough to play Test cricket for England. At Old Trafford it had been all disappointment, all frustration, all resentment. Now at

Lord's, I quaked at the thought that in a few minutes time I would be part of an England team in action.

There was something more to worry about than natural diffidence: six days earlier, on a pig of a wicket at Middlesbrough, we had beaten Gloucestershire by an innings before six o'clock on the second day and Mike Procter, bowling like an express train, had hit me on the little finger of my left hand. To this day I cannot move that finger inwards to meet the third finger and on 26 June 1969, it hurt like hell. I had declared myself fit to play because I wanted so badly to play, but I wasn't fit. Now, to all my doubts about my own ability was added the fear that I might drop a catch. Then everyone would know I had gone into a Test with a finger so badly damaged that I was a liability in the field. I would never be picked again. Please, oh please, don't let a catch go to that left hand. My fears multiplied as Illy said, 'Go to leg slip, Hamp', and with a little inward groan and another muttered prayer I took up station. There was no cause for alarm for quite a while as Steve Camacho and Roy Fredericks put on 106 together for the first wicket but that didn't give me any peace of mind at all, because every ball was potentially a catch coming my way. I crouched, shivering because it was a sweater day and everyone was wearing one except me, sweating because of the terrible knowledge of a throbbing finger and the possibility of a catch seeking it out. At last it came.

Now the time it takes for a ball to fly from the edge of the bat to a fieldsman standing perhaps 15 yards back is about the time it takes to blink an eye. Certainly you can't measure it on a watch. And the time it takes for a conscious thought to form in the mind and be analysed must be a good deal longer. That, logic tells me, is a simple fact of life. But enough thoughts flashed through my mind as the ball was on its way to me to fill a diary: it *mustn't* go to my left hand . . . I must, somehow, get the right hand to it whatever its line . . . I must use the left to fold round and complete the catch . . . if I dropped it I was exposed to the whole world as a man who went into a Test when he was unfit. I heard the cries of 'catch it', first from Barry Knight, who had brought one back up the hill to the left-handed Fredericks, echoed by the slips. I even heard Boycott at mid-wicket join in: 'Hold it, Hamp!' Until that moment I had regarded it as a meaningless figure-of-speech to say that a man's whole life flashes through his mind in certain circumstances. I realised then that it is no idle metaphor. The whole of my life flashed before me. The ball went, thank God, to my right hand. It bounced up, and as it came down the left hand closed round it and all was con-gratulations. The first ordeal was over.

Later in the innings I reached up to take a catch off Basil Butcher as he hooked David Brown. Yes, the first ordeal was over. The next came late on the second day, after West Indies had totalled 380. John Edrich was out for 7, Peter Parfitt for 4, Basil d'Oliveira without scoring, and suddenly we were in very real danger of following on. 19 for 1, 37 for 2, 37 for 3 and then – oh, my God! – 37 for 4 as Boycott was out and I had to go in to bat in a Test for the first time before a full house at Lord's with the more vocal section of the crowd bay-ing for blood. On that long walk out to the middle I had to pass Sobers, waiting to bowl, and my partner, Philip Sharpe, gazing with huge eyes from that moon-rise face. I took guard, asking myself what I was doing there, and Sobers hurtled in. I felt and heard, rather than saw, the first ball whistle past my left ear and Gary, following right through until he was half a yard away from me, showed me the smile on the face of the tiger as he said pleasantly, 'Evening, Hamp.' Somehow we got through to close of play and as we climbed back to the dressing room I saw one of those sights which somehow stays forever in the mind: John Snow, no. 11, with his pads on! 'Charming,' I thought. 'That's confidence for you.' Thoughts of night-watchmen didn't occur to me.

Next morning we carried on and just when Sharpie seemed

to be settling, he got a beauty from Holder and was out for 11 – 61 for 5 and the follow-on looming starkly before us. But Alan Knott stayed until we just – only just – saved the follow-on and in came my captain to talk of our next tactical goal: getting close enough to the Windies total to make defeat impossible and victory a possibility. I read later that I reached a first Test hundred in my first Test, and at headquarters, by 'running the ball down to third man'. I've never 'run' a ball down to third man in my life; it was an edge, like a lot more edges I got in that innings. There are players who will be generous and say that it wasn't a bad innings at all. Frankly, I can't remember all that much about it – I seemed to bat in some sort of daze – but I do recall a lot of edges. What I remember with great clarity is disappointment at being given out lbw at 107. It didn't seem a good decision at all but looking back over the years, Lord's on a Saturday was not a bad place or time to get a maiden Test hundred.

During the innings I took a knock on the forearm and at the end of the Test I went for a check-up. The X-ray revealed a hairline fracture, and another on the finger damaged by Procter before the Test. I had scored my maiden Test hundred with both those fractures.

I scored 1 and 22 in the Third test and was dropped for the first of the new three-match series against New Zealand, starting on 24 July. Between the first and second of those Tests I received a letter from Alec Bedser in which he advised me to keep my right shoulder 'behind' my left to avoid hitting across the ball. He also told me that he would be watching keenly for some runs and that I should not for one moment think I was forgotten or discarded. During August I had scores of 62 against Lancashire, 93 against Notts, 85 against Somerset, 63 against Surrey, 57 against Kent and 45 against Leicestershire but I did not play in a Test against New Zealand. I must have hit those 400-odd runs, not to mention that hundred at Lord's, with my shoulders in the wrong place.

10

An Era Ends . . .

Yorkshire's annual report for the year 1968 included three moderately phrased but highly significant sentences: 'D. B. Close is again thanked for his inspiring leadership of the team'; 'Your Committee regrets that the time has come for the great-hearted Freddie Trueman to retire'; 'Your Committee also regrets that K. Taylor has retired . . . and that R. Illingworth has decided to leave the County Team, especially as his decision is due to dissatisfaction with the terms of his engagement.'

The significance of the first sentence will be seen later; the second needs no amplification; the third is just a trifle misleading, or at any rate open to misinterpretation. In recent years, especially when the pro-Boycott, anti-Illingworth faction amongst Yorkshire members became more vocal in the late 'seventies and early 'eighties, an impression has grown that Illy left Yorkshire for Leicestershire to get more money, or because Yorkshire would not pay him more. That is completely false. If Leicestershire valued Raymond's services more highly than Yorkshire had done, then that is their affair. Certainly they got full value for money, whatever they paid him. But wild horses would never have prised Raymond Illingworth loose from his Yorkshire roots if the county committee had not refused to acknowledge that times were changing. What Raymond asked for was a little more security than that offered by a simple gentleman's agreement between county and player which was renewed (or not) once

68

a year. In fact, Illingworth firmly believed in the same pay for all capped players, reasoning (in a way which all of us understood) that although he was not worth the same money as Hutton and the rest when he first arrived in the team, and neither were young players like myself to be compared with him when we were first capped, it evened out in a good, democratic way and you were not likely to be capped in those days unless a lot of people were convinced that you were good, that you were going to get better and that you would remain so for quite a long time. What Ray wanted was a contract for two or three years which gave a young man with a growing family a sense of security. If a player felt himself going downhill it would not be difficult to sense the feeling in the camp and to know whether or not he was likely to be re-engaged for the following season. Thus he would have some time to work out his future plans. To discover, suddenly, at the end of a season that there was to be no place for him in the club in the following season was a very different matter.

I think it's fair to say that everyone in the team understood Illy's point of view. The trouble was that no-one on the committee did, least of all the all-powerful chairman, Brian Sellers. For the man whose image as county captain had been that of the Great Democrat, the man who could out-cuss 'Ticker' Mitchell if the necessity arose and who prided himself on calling spades bloody shovels, Sellers became the Great Autocrat as chairman of the club. You did as he said, or else. And to be painfully frank about it, his thinking was that of an age long since gone by. Cricketers in the 1960s were for the most part better educated than those of the 'twenties and 'thirties. Yet their pay and standing in the community was not what it had been, in relative terms, in Sellers' days. Nor were the modern players he ruled with his iron rod the forelock-touching brigade he seemed to think they should be.

When Illy, driven by lack of sympathetic response from the committee to his request for a contract, was forced to give an ultimatum – 'a contract or I quit' – the Sellers response was, sadly, predictable: 'Let him go, then, and he can take any other bugger who feels t' same way.' Illingworth left for Leicestershire, where he became their captain and led them out of 90 years in cricket's wilderness to a County Championship in 1975, Benson and Hedges Cup victories in 1972 and 1975 and John Player League championships in 1974 and 1977.

But if his move brought the first successes in the whole history of Leicestershire cricket it also brought about, more than any other one factor, the downfall of Yorkshire cricket. Of that there is no doubt whatsoever.

Ray Illingworth and Brian Close had been friends since their earliest days in the Yorkshire nets. They were born within five or six miles of each other. They had served their apprenticeship in the stern competition of the Bradford League which, when they were boys, provided great cricket and produced a seemingly endless stream of players not only for Yorkshire but for almost every other first-class county. Closey had been best man at Illy's wedding. Their personal liking for each other was of the variety which made it always possible for them to criticise each other in colourful and trenchant terms and still remain the best of friends. Their professional respect for each other was as total as it was profound. In short, they made a truly great team.

Ray Illingworth and Brian Close were two of the greatest cricketers I have ever known and each, in his different way, was a brilliant captain. Close had the dash, the flair. He would introduce fielding changes which seemed to possess no cricket logic at all and yet produced a wicket. He would make a bowling change which defied all rational thinking and break a seemingly unbreakable stand. When Yorkshire were attacking in the field, pressing for a win which to the rest of the cricketing world seemed improbable in the extreme, he was a dynamic and inspiring leader. And he led always by example by going first into the utterly suicidal fielding positions. The genial Don Wilson, who knew his limitations as a slow left-arm bowler, used to gulp and turn white as Closey stationed himself two yards from the bat of a batsman of known quality on a slow, non-turning wicket. He was battered and bloodied for year after year but he never flinched, never took evasive action. That furrowed brow, that determined and ferocious scowl, was always there at the batsman's elbow – left or right.

Raymond Illingworth, by contrast, was the ice-cold calcu-lating brain of cricket. Like Closey, he knew every man in the game, knew his weaknesses, but unlike Close, Illingworth respected a player's strengths as well. Close concentrated all his thinking on attacking a batsman's vulnerability without regard for his talent. Illingworth reasoned that everyone was going to succeed against York-shire some time, and his genius lay in making life as difficult as possible for any batsman who started to dominate. Close believed that no-one should ever dominate in a game against Yorkshire; Illingworth's reasoning legislated for that possi-bility. So when the unthinkable (as far as Closey was con-cerned) occasionally happened, and the opposition started to take control, Jimmy Binks' rallying cry from behind the stumps was heard: 'Hey up. T'rudder's gone. Come and take control, Illy.' Then sometimes quietly, sometimes with a furious exchange between captain and first lieutenant, Illing-worth would start to work things out. And when the tumult and shouting had died and the ship was on an even keel once more, no-one was diminished, no-one had lost face. It was a team effort led by one or other or both of the best brains in cricket.

In essence, Illingworth was utterly indispensable, not only to the team but to Closey himself. When two years later it was Close's turn to leave the county, he had an immediate and handsome approach from Leicestershire and he was given this advice: 'Raymond was a marvellous lieutenant to you with Yorkshire. How do you think you would be as a lieutenant to him?' For once in his life, Brian took the hint and the advice implicit in it. He went to a new command in Somerset and in his turn led them out of 90 years in the wilderness to become a major force in English cricket. His influence can still be seen in the person of Ian Botham – so much God-given talent allied to the aggression and disdain for the opposition which constituted the D. B. Close trademark.

But Illingworth's influence on Close was not limited to events on the field. Close would listen with respect and understanding to very few people, but Raymond was high on the list of those he would listen to. If Illingworth had stayed with Yorkshire, Close's supreme and oft-broadcast contempt for the one-day competitions in general, and the John Player League in particular, would have been under some restraint. Illy would quite simply have told his captain to 'bloody well shut up' when Close was about to embark on yet another tirade against the damage that limited-overs cricket was doing to the first-class game. The trouble with Close was that he cared so deeply for county and Test cricket that it represented his whole world and anything that was likely to have an adverse effect upon it was total anathema to him. Illy, the pragmatist, liked one-day cricket no more than Close did – indeed, as a specialist slow bowler, he was entitled to like it a good deal less than Close did – but he recognised the need for it in purely financial terms. That is the view of most first-class cricketers, but with dear old Closey there have never been any grey areas; it's either good or bad for the game, and one-day cricket, as he saw it, was very, very bad.

It would have been all right for him to take this view if he had kept his violent opinions privately inside those circles where they were understood and where he could always expect to find sympathy for them. But Closey has never been strong in tact or discretion. He trumpeted his denunciations from every rampart of cricket. 'Instant rubbish' became his battle hymn, and it put him on a collision course with Brian Sellers.

It is difficult to conceive Brian Sellers' views on the John Player League Sunday slog being very different from those so often and so colourfully expressed by Close (who in many ways was very like Sellers), but that was not really the point as far as the club chairman was concerned. Whether we liked it or not, this was a competition now played by first-class counties and so Yorkshire had not only to be good at it, they had to be the best. It did not help matters as far as the chairman was concerned, I'm quite sure, that the John Player League was won in each of its first two years by Lancashire. It might be a load of crash-bang-wallop rubbish, but if that lot across the Pennines could win it, then by hell Yorkshire simply had to win it. In 1969 we finished eighth in the table with seven wins from 16 games, but as we won the Gillette Cup in an uninspiring final with Derbyshire (though notable for the Man of the Match award going to an uncapped Yorkshireman, Barry Leadbeater), the modest performance in the other one-day competition passed without undue comment. The annual report this year, however, merely 'thanked' Close for his leadership with no suggestion that it was 'inspiring'.

In 1970 we managed just five John Player League wins to finish fourteenth, and we were bowled out for 76 by Surrey at Harrogate to exit from the Gillette Cup in the first round. The lack of success in the one-day competitions, which were now acknowledged money-spinners to gladden the hearts of county treasurers, was allied to the cancellation of the South African cricket tour to produce what the committee described as 'financially, the most disastrous season in the history of the Club.' Someone had to shoulder the blame, even if some of the causes were far outside his personal province, and so: 'After long and careful consideration, the Committee decided not to re-appoint D. B. Close as first-team captain for 1971 and in view of this decision, it was also decided that he should no longer be a playing member of the team.'

That's the formal version of Close's sacking. In real terms, he was called from his home by a telephone call and drove to Headingley, thinking it was a routine committee meeting. He was given five minutes to decide whether he would resign or be sacked. There was something brutally mediaeval about that ultimatum. It broke Close's heart.

He had played for Yorkshire since he was 18, in 1949. He had played Test cricket for England before he had won his Yorkshire cap. He had scored 22,650 runs, taken 967 wickets, been hammered black and blue both as a batsman and a fielder. He had captained England seven times without being beaten. He had led Yorkshire for eight seasons during which we had won four County Championships and two Gillette Cups. Since his departure, Yorkshire have never looked remotely like winning another thing. Never before, in well over 100 years of Yorkshire cricket, have seven lean years been followed by seven more.

It is impossible to rid oneself of the feeling that in a way, Close brought it upon himself. His violent opposition to one-day cricket, his public denunciation of it, was unrealistic in the economic climate of 1970. It must have seemed wildly illogical to the Yorkshire committee that in what was financially their most disastrous year, their captain was hell-bent on killing the one goose which laid golden eggs. Close's refusal to look at limited-overs cricket as anything other than a playing disaster must have seemed to the committee to be closely linked to the county's failure to make any sort of mark in that type of game in that black year. They put two and two together, came up with an answer of about 64 and took action accordingly. They summarily dismissed one of their greatest servants, a great cricketer, a superb captain, a man who would have died for Yorkshire cricket (and, as he has written himself, damned nearly did so on many occasions), a player whose genius was often flawed and erratic but who possessed genius nonetheless, a man whose thinking alternated wildly between astonishingly brilliant and just plain daft.

But if Illingworth had not left in 1968, Close would not have left in 1970. Without the sobering and responsible restraint of the first lieutenant, the captain sailed a course to disaster – for himself and for Yorkshire. It was tragedy enough for any county to lose two such cricket brains in two years; it was a catastrophe of the highest magnitude that the double loss should be a matter of cause and effect.

Freddie Trueman's incomparable career came to a close in 1968 and that was the end of an era for Yorkshire cricket. He had joined the side for the first time in the same game as Close, back in 1949, and he had bowled with pace, hostility and character for 20 seasons. In some ways it was a relief to see him go out still at the top, with the greatest triumph of his life still fresh in his mind: Yorkshire's victory over the Australian tourists at Bramall Lane, flamboyantly accomplished under Fred's bloodthirsty leadership on 2 July 1968. Age had begun to take its toll, even on the utterly irrepressible FST, at the age of 38, and we would all of us have hated to see the great man getting collared by lesser mortals as we remembered the world-class players he had overwhelmed in his time. We were conscious that in 115 years of Yorkshire cricket there had been only one Fred; we were grateful, eternally grateful, to have played alongside him, and we were now resigned to the fact that it might be another 115 years before another Trueman came along. At least his departure, irreplaceable though he was, was something we accepted as being in the natural order of things. So, in a different dimension, was Ken Taylor's retirement; a dogged batsman, a very useful bits-and-pieces bowler, Ken was a cover point fieldsman to rank with Colin Bland and Clive Lloyd. Put together with Illy's move to Leicestershire, these changes meant we had enormous gaps to fill in our front-line ranks. Then in 1969, Jimmy Binks retired – the third member of Yorkshire's War Cabinet – and in strategy and tactics D. B. Close now stood alone. Twelve months later, the lightning struck him down.

I heard the news of Closey's sacking in Brisbane, on tour with MCC in company with Boycott and Wilson. Yorkshire had telephoned Boycott to offer him the captaincy and Wilson the vice-captaincy. My first reaction was to feel pleased for Boycott and very, very sorry for Closey. Although I reasoned that he had to some extent brought it on himself by ignoring the storm clouds which had been gathering for two or three years and drifting across the broad expanse of sky between Brian Sellers and Brian Close, the thought that he was now completely out of Yorkshire cricket seemed to me unnecessarily severe and cruel. But it was there, it was done and now was the time to ponder the future. Although I was pleased for his sake, I was frankly surprised by Boycott's appointment. Philip Sharpe, then Richard Hutton, seemed more logical choices and my own best bet would have been Duggie Padgett, now the senior player on the books, respected and liked by everyone and someone who got on well with every member of the side. But he, like Hutton and Sharpe, had been passed over. Geoffrey Boycott was the new captain and I wondered what the next decade of Yorkshire cricket was going to be like.

Before that new era began, there was still the matter of the tour in which we were involved and there is no doubt that it had a significant effect upon Geoffrey Boycott's career, if not mine. This is my story, true, but so far it had run quietly parallel to Boycott's. We were from roughly the same area, had roughly the same cricketing backgrounds and as far as I have always been concerned, there the resemblances and connections ended. I had always got along perfectly well with him. Indeed, there had been no reason, so far as I was concerned, why that should not be. He was now to be my county captain and the committee's decision was mildly surprising to me – not for any personal reason whatsoever, but because it seemed to me that seniority had been ignored. But as I had not seen myself in the slightest degree as a candidate for the captaincy, it was not a matter to give me cause for deep reflection. I did not foresee any major problems; certainly I did not anticipate the crises which were to overtake York-shire in the next ten years and in no way at all did I dream that I would be mixed up in them in a terribly personal way. Looking back, I can honestly say that the thought never entered my head that the cricket careers of Geoff and myself, which had run their side-by-side course with such tranquility for so long were now on an inevitable collision course.

On the winter tour of 1970–71 we were England, as well as Yorkshire, team-mates. No more, no less. I knew of course, as we all did, that Geoff was keenly interested in personal records. That was the way he was made, he was not the first man to be so inclined and he certainly won't be the last. He was probably round about his peak at that time, a very fine batsman indeed, and it is more than likely that Wally Hammond's record of 1553 runs in a tour to Australia was in his mind, especially as he, along with John Edrich and Brian Luckhurst, had a superb tour. But in the very first match, against South Australia in Adelaide, Barry Richards (guest-ing for the State side) had made a huge score against us and Geoff was well on his way to a massive reply when Ray Illingworth, the tour captain, asked him to 'get on with it' when play resumed the following morning. Geoff got out fairly early, and was not pleased. Whether it was the captain's orders which brought about his dismissal, or just one of those things that happen to all of us, I don't know. I do know that he was certainly a bit peeved about getting out. Then came the bat-throwing incident, again at Adelaide, but this time in the Test. He'd reached 58 when Max O'Connell, something of a controversial umpire on that tour, gave him run out and I was one of those who thought he wasn't out. It was one of those 50-50 decisions with half the side, watching from square on, feeling that Geoff was out and the other half taking the opposite view. Looking back when he had run past the wicket, Geoff was in no doubt at all and threw down his bat in disgust. At once there was all hell let loose on TV, on the radio and in the newspapers – and more immediately on the field, with the Aussies giving him a severe dose of 'the verbals'. Now I'm not a demonstrative player myself and I can't say I enjoy demonstrations and ostentatious dissent. But at the same time I have never been able to see why such gestures by batsmen generate so much more heat than those by bowlers. Throughout the ages, bowlers have let off steam when umpiring decisions have gone against them, fast bowlers in particular, and I suppose one of my heroes, F. S. Trueman, was among the worst offenders. Fred these days is an altogether respectable figure in the commentary box and pronounces himself firmly against the questioning of umpires' decisions, and I am sure he firmly believes now that in his heyday he was whiter than white. But all those who played with and against him will readily vouch for the fact that he was known to question not only the umpire's decision but his parentage, character and antecedents as well. That led (along, of course, with his magnificent bowling) to the building of one of cricket's legendary characters. If his explosive nature gave him a kind of heroism, why does a similar trait spell villainy when exhibited by a batsman? I've always wondered. Geoff's peace of mind was hardly restored when Raymond found it necessary to apologise for his leading batsman's conduct.

Then came the unkindest cut of all. Just 18 runs short of breaking Hammond's record and with the Test in Sydney coming up, Boycott had to play in a one-day game and Graham McKenzie broke his forearm. Gone was the chance of a record which I am sure Boycott dearly wanted, and he had to return to England before the end of the tour. I remember it well because he had let his hair grow a bit, counting on getting it trimmed when we moved on to New Zealand. In the haste of last-minute arrangements for his flight home, there was not even time to visit a barber's shop and I ended up cutting the Boycott locks and trimming the neck-hair with an electric razor. Perhaps a couple of Yorkshiremen enjoyed the thought of saving a dollar or two in that way!

On the other side of the world, 15,000 miles away, the summary dismissal of Brian Close had created a tremendous furore in Yorkshire and a Reform Group had been active in the club while we had been in Australia. By the time we returned, most of the tumult and shouting had died. There was an air of official optimism that under new management, so to speak, business would continue as usual – and in Yorkshire cricket, normal business means first of all winning the County Championship and then picking up any minor honours which came along. Looked at realistically, such optimism was quite absurd. No side could lose players of the calibre of Illingworth, Trueman, Binks and then Close without having its efficiency savagely impaired. We had a nucleus of experience in Boycott, Padgett, Sharpe, Nicholson, Hutton, Wilson and myself; a cadre of semi-seasoned players like Balderstone, Bairstow, Old, Leadbeater and Cope; and then a handful of youngsters who, it was hoped, would be the stars of the future in Colin Johnson, Andrew Dalton, Peter Squires, Howard Cooper, Phil Carrick, Richard Lumb, John Woodford, Arthur Robinson and Mike Bore. There was an immense amount of potential if you looked at the names through the eyes of a 1971 official. All were players of good pedigree and high promise. Yet how many of them came through to establish themselves as regular first-team players? How many of them came even close to equalling the performances of the men who had gone before?

Of the seven who formed the hard core of seasoned professionalism, five had drifted away for various reasons by the middle of the 'seventies and only Boycott and myself remained, so in seven years, Yorkshire lost Taylor, Sharpe, Padgett, Close, Illingworth, Hutton, Binks, Wilson, Trueman and Nicholson – nine Test players and the best bowler of his time not to be capped by his country. If you went out and picked a Yorkshire League or Bradford League player at random to make up the numbers, together with those ten names, you would have a side to beat any first-class county, then or now. Did no-one see the danger signals? Through a hundred years Yorkshire had carefully, almost suspiciously, introduced new players very, very gently into sides composed already of great men. Having served honourable and distinguished terms, those stars were finally bowed out with the club confident and secure in its knowledge that replacements destined for equal, or even greater, glory were to hand. And yet here, in seven short years, one of the finest sides of all time was allowed to disintegrate before even two or three potential replacements were knocking on the dressing room door. Can there ever have been such appalling mismanagement or misjudgement? I seem to remember saying at the time that it would take Yorkshire ten years to recover from the loss of so many fine players. Well, those ten years have come and gone with still no real sign of a recovery.

I have already paid tribute to the contribution made by Taylor, Trueman, Illingworth, Binks and Close. Duggie Padgett, who would have been my logical choice as captain to succeed Close, had played for Yorkshire since 1951. He was still 44 days short of his seventeenth birthday when he scored 25 not out in an innings victory over Somerset but, typical of Yorkshire's careful system of 'blooding' young players, he did not play again for six weeks and that was the extent of his first-team experience for 1951. Duggie was what you would call 'a reight Bradford lad'. He had a homely accent, a simple taste in food (only demanding plenty of it), a genuine affection for a good pint of bitter and a disturbing tendency to walk and talk in his sleep. He was not, I think, a great theorist about the game which may be a little surprising considering the amount of time he spent in the company of Ray Illingworth. For many years they drove from match to match together and shared a room. It says much for Illy's real affection for Duggie that this partnership continued over so many years because Raymond was a man who insisted on getting his required amount of sleep while 'Padg' would frequently leap up in the middle of the night, arms aloft, yelling 'How's that?' Padgett was an honest, modest soul of whom it was said, when he first came into the Yorkshire side, 'He looks more like Hutton than Hutton.' He certainly had all the strokes and made them with the elegance and charm of a Tom Graveney. His cutting in particular was beautifully timed, and he played the late cut better than anyone in his day. Doug was not a wildly ambitious man. His philosophy was quite straightforward: he had a summer job which he loved and which he could do well. He just needed some winter work to get him through to next summer and he was content. I spent the 1963 season as his opening partner and in the Yorkshire way of those days we then travelled together, ate together and relaxed together so that we developed a pretty good understanding of each other. Duggie was a completely down-to-earth, utterly straightforward chap and I don't think there was anyone in first-class cricket who didn't like him. He scored more than 20,000 runs for Yorkshire and played twice for England.

Philip Sharpe was an entirely different character, no less likeable than Padgett but a much more lively personality, deeply involved with life. He developed a close association with Don Wilson and Richard Hutton and what a marvellously contrasting trio they were. Sharpe was perhaps the quietest man in a very noisy dressing room, usually poring over a crossword puzzle, but off-duty in the evenings he was undoubtedly the noisiest. That is perhaps an unkind way to put it because the noise he generated took the form of singing, which he invariably led. The team had a close and delightful relationship with the Black and White Minstrels in the 1960s and in London or Scarborough, depending upon where the company was playing, we spent a lot of happy hours with men like Dai Francis and Tony Mercer and John Boulter. We developed our own repertoire of the B & W routines and could sing them for hours. P. J. Sharpe was inevitably in the van. As a batsman, he had his own distinctive method and punched the ball into the covers with a characteristic forearm jab. He scored 17,600 runs for Yorkshire and in his 12 Tests averaged 46.23 for England, as well as holding 17 slip catches. It was in this area that 'the little fat guy', or 'Toby Jug', was in a class of his own. In 1962 he held 71 catches at slip, and whether it was the first over of the day or the last, his concentration never seemed to lapse for a second. If he had played more Tests, I am pretty certain I would have rated him above Bobby Simpson as the greatest of all slip-catchers at all levels.

Richard Hutton was an altogether different type. His humour was of a lugubrious type, uttered in sepulchral tones and usually with an air of lofty disdain. His cricket pedigree was of course impeccable, and he joined Yorkshire with the self-confidence born of a successful schoolboy career at Repton and three distinguished years with Cambridge

University. If he was impressed by the professional greatness about him, he showed no sign of it and Hutton it was who came closest to having the last word in what is now a famous exchange with F. S. Trueman:

Trueman: '. . . and I bowled one which pitched middle and leg and just missed t'top o' t'off stick.'

Hutton: 'Tell me, Fred, have you ever bowled a ball which merely went straight?'

Trueman, with lightning riposte: 'Aye, three year ago. It were a full toss and knocked Peter Marner's middle hob out like a streak o' piss.'

Nice try, Richard.

Hutton was a very good fast bowler indeed, capable of producing the unplayable delivery in Trueman style if not, perhaps, with quite the same frequency. He had a seemingly lazy, indolent approach to life which was deceiving. It deceived Brian Sellers to the extent that when he despatched Richard to play for Yorkshire for the first time in the Old Trafford Roses match of 1962, he sent a special message to the captain, Vic Wilson: 'Keep an eye on young Hutton or he might wander off into t'crowd and get lost.' Hutton scored nearly 5000 runs for Yorkshire, took 468 wickets and I don't think really did full justice to his all-round ability in his five Test matches.

Don Wilson was a marvellous character. He was, I believe, the most expectant bowler the game has ever seen, sometimes crouching, sometimes leaping after delivering the ball, arms flailing all over the place as he quite genuinely expected a wicket from every single delivery. He was not the greatest slow left-armer in the great Yorkshire dynasty of bowlers of that type but he had a marvellously infectious enthusiasm for the game, loved to laugh almost as much as he loved to win and was a great man to have in a dressing room. When he was fielding at mid-wicket with Ken Taylor at cover, Yorkshire's outcricket was something wonderful to see and between them they saved literally hundreds of runs. As a left-hand batsman, 'Wils' loved to hit sixes even more than the average tail-ender. At Bramall Lane in 1960, he went in to face a Surrey attack which included Alec Bedser, Peter Loader and Tony Lock, with a scoreboard showing Yorkshire at 65 for 5 on a rain-affected pitch. He hit a marvellously spectacular 83, by far his career-best up to that point, and went out in search of the car registration plate which he finally acquired: DON 83. Wilson spent several winters of distinguished coaching in South Africa and returned to be the chief coach at the MCC School at Lord's: an unlikely climax, perhaps, to the career of the only Yorkshire cricketer to come out of the Dales, but a richly deserved reward because Wilson developed into a magnificent coach. He took more than 1100 wickets for Yorkshire, hit 5788 runs and had three hat-tricks.

Tony Nicholson was quite simply the best bowler of his day never to play for England. He had to withdraw from the party selected to tour South Africa in 1964–65, otherwise I am sure he would have won a Test place and kept it for a long time. From a rather ungainly delivery stride he bowled a magnificent late outswinger and, after his first season of learning his trade, he combined this method of attack by cutting the ball back off the seam. Here was another marvellous extrovert character. 'Nick' returned from a spell in Rhodesia with his parents to the county in which he had been born. Unlike the rest of us, he had not only lived abroad, he had worked abroad, and in the relatively colourful role of a policeman. Each recounting of his life patrolling his beat on horseback became more colourful in the telling but no-one begrudged Nick a bit of licence. He was a wholly likeable character, a big teddy bear of a man who, while not a fast bowler in the Trueman sense, developed all the quicker man's aggression. The refusal of an lbw appeal would immediately result in the adoption of what became known throughout the game as 'Nick's teapot stance'. He would stand, a picture of utter disgust, with right hand on hip and head nodding up and down as he ground out words of disbelief, of disgust, of despair. There would be much shaking of the head, a world of reproach in the glance directed at the umpire as he trudged sadly back to try again. He used to count up the number of refusals he had suffered at the hands of each umpire on the circuit and keep a sort of league table in his head which was always topped by Tommy Spencer. The mere sight of Tommy arriving at a ground was enough to wring a groan of despair from A. G. Nicholson. And yet I am absolutely certain that no umpire in the game ever felt a moment's resentment about these performances. Nick was entirely without malice, had the heart of a lion and would bowl all day on the best wicket in the world if that was what his captain wanted. He took 876 wickets for Yorkshire at fewer than 20 runs apiece, was rated more highly by Fred Trueman than any other of his 40 opening partners, and was respected by every batsman in the game.

Sadly, his career ended through serious illness, stemming from injuries to his legs which had pounded so willingly up and down the cricket grounds of England for 13 years. Twice he nearly died. It is quite characteristic of Nick that today he strides the golf courses of the North, his smile beaming upon the world, his infectious chuckle audible across a couple of fairways and the teapot stance seen again when a putt refuses to go into the hole!

Like many of us, he was becoming a little disenchanted with life as a Yorkshire cricketer when illness struck him down and for a long time after his recovery he kept away from the dressing room. When he finally did pay a visit, in 1981, and offered a bit of friendly advice to a current practitioner of his own art, he was snubbed: 'You don't know anything about it. It's a different game today.'

Padgett, Sharpe, Hutton, Wilson, Nicholson: these were

the men Yorkshire had to replace after already losing Taylor, Illingworth, Trueman, Binks and Close. Of the five, only Nicholson's departure was due to ill health. The others need not have left when they did. Although Sellers had abdicated as absolute monarch, his dictum seemed still to be county policy: 'Let him go, and take any other bugger who wants to go.' There was a death wish in Yorkshire's administrative policy in the 'seventies, which is why that young man in the Yorkshire dressing room was right. It *is* a different game. Not a better one, but it's different, right enough.

11

... A Nightmare Begins

The summer of 1971 produced, according to the county's annual report, 'the worst season in the history of the Club, without doubt, both from a playing and a financial point of view.' It also produced the finest seasonal playing record of Geoffrey Boycott's Yorkshire career: 2,221 runs from 25 innings and an average of 105.6.

There you have straightaway the pattern developing which was to cause an enormous rift in the ranks of Yorkshire members, a rift which was to continue throughout the 'seventies and into the next decade. In 1983 it shows not the slightest sign of being repaired. It is one of the greatest tragedies in the whole history of the game everywhere and, in the particular context of Yorkshire cricket, the ultimate tragedy. The basic cause of the rift was the feeling amongst Geoff's supporters – there were and are many of them – that he was an outstandingly good player who was consistently let down by the other players round about him. They see no wrong in anything he does and very little right in the performances of anyone else. Fair enough. They are entitled to their view and they can produce a mass of entirely valid statistics to back it up, although figures on their own can be grossly misleading. For example, the basic premise that Geoff was very, very good and the rest very, very poor is an extremely dangerous and misleading over-simplification.

No-one in 1971 could say that the career records of Sharpe, Hutton, Padgett, Wilson, Nicholson and myself merited a rating of anything less than respectable. If some of those records began to take on a less distinguished appearance from 1971 onwards one has to start looking for an explanation. It wasn't just an accident; it wasn't a coincidence; it wasn't a matter of six very fair players all losing form simultaneously for no accountable reason.

It was never going to be easy for Boycott to take over as captain and it was especially unfortunate that his broken arm had not fully healed by the time the season started. He was a natural loner and had been since first coming into the Yorkshire side. He was virtually a non-drinker and no-one thought any the less of him for that, but it naturally limited his opportunities of joining in the fun of off-duty periods – and there had been a great deal of fun in the 'sixties. In that time, too, a lot of close friendships had developed – Sharpe–Hutton–Wilson, Padgett and myself, Nick with all of us – and they certainly were not going to change. As just another member of the side and doing his own thing, Boycott had not concerned himself about these group friendships. As a captain, and particularly if things were going wrong, it was more or less inevitable that he would now come to look upon the groups as cliques, and on occasions I'm sure he felt that one or another of them were ganging up on him. For example, there was no disguising – indeed, no attempt was made to disguise it – Hutton's personal dislike of Boycott. You might even say it bordered upon contempt. Sharpe wasn't and isn't an aggressive type of personality so there was nothing from him like Hutton's antipathy. But Boycott, I'm sure, would feel that Sharpe didn't look upon him as any sort of kindred spirit. Wilson was his vice-captain but he was also a close friend of Hutton and Sharpe. No, it was never going to be easy.

Close's dictum on captaincy was that you had to *give* – to

give everything of yourself to your team. Boycott could give nothing of himself. He was just made that way, a loner, desperately wanting to be liked but finding himself unable to achieve popularity except through his ability to score runs. I am absolutely sure he believed, and still believes, that massive scoring is in itself a passport to universal popularity.

To be fair to Boycott, he did make an obvious effort to get closer to his team than he had been as just one of them. When we were invited by a county to its committee room for a drink after the day's play he obviously went as the captain of the side, but on other occasions, such as our visits to the Original Oak, near Headingley, he started to join in as he had not done previously. Clearly he was trying, and it cannot have been easy for him, sitting on the sidelines as we started 1971 with a crushing defeat at the hands of Kent at Park Avenue. With Boycott injured, Wilson in the new appointment of vice-captain (previously the senior professional had simply stood in when the captain was out of the side) took over the leadership, but somehow he never regained the confidence which had won him a tour of Australia. There is a school of thought that Wilson was not nearly as good a bowler without Close as his captain and it is certainly true that he suffered from not having Ray Illingworth at the other end. By 1972 his bowling had deteriorated to an alarming extent and in 1971 it was nowhere near as effective as it had been under the previous regime. And, good lad though he was, Wils was not a particularly successful captain. The whole scene had changed, the whole script was different, the actors on stage seemed different people.

The leading players gradually formed two camps and the supporting cast of junior players – more of them than Yorkshire were accustomed to having on stage at any one time but still, in 1971, prepared to learn from the principals – must have watched in horror and formed their own impressions of who was right and who was wrong. On the one hand, Boycott standing virtually alone; on the other, Hutton, Sharpe and Wilson, believing firmly in Yorkshire but looking at things from an entirely different point of view from the captain; in the middle, more or less, myself and Nicholson who would both dearly have loved to bring everyone together but were unable for the life of us to see just how that could be done. Boycott, in his moments of self-imposed torment, would confide in us his distress and resentment at what he regarded as disloyalty from the trio. Over a drink in the evening, the same trio would voice their outrage at a man who in their eyes put his individual achievements before the performance of the team or the results it achieved. I was not at that stage wholly convinced by their arguments. At the same time, they were friends of ten years standing, ten good years in which Boycott had had every chance to enjoy the same sort of camaraderie if he had opted to do so, and without taking sides, neither Nick nor I was going to abandon friendships which we valued.

Now that may sound rather more clear-cut than it really was. There was no obvious open breach, no overt taking of sides or forming of different camps in the dressing room. Above all, we were a team, and while it might not have looked a very united or integrated team at times, its members at least tried to pull together when involved in a game. The differences were rather more philosophical than anything else. Boycott just didn't think like Hutton, Sharpe and Wilson (and, come to think of it, on a lot of subjects that whimsical trio didn't think much alike either!) so it was difficult to find any sort of common ground. They did not openly oppose him in any way which would have undermined his authority with younger players and generally their strictures were reserved for the sort of private occasions when we were off-duty. No more did Tony Nicholson or I give any indication of siding with either faction – indeed, we didn't side with either. We just wanted everyone to get on with the job of playing cricket for Yorkshire, but we were damned if either of us could think of a way of getting everyone on the same wavelength.

Let me add that Hutton and Co. were not against everything Boycott did by any means, so there was no sort of running feud. There would be times when Nick or I felt more strongly about something Geoff had said or done than, say, Sharpe or Wilson. It was never a question of them-and-us (or, on the outside looking in as I felt I was, perhaps them-and-them is a better expression). It wasn't easy to define but somehow it was neither healthy nor wholesome.

Geoff came back into the side for our second match in 1971, possibly earlier than was wise as far as his injured arm was concerned, and promptly started getting runs – lots of runs. But to win matches it is necessary to bowl the other side out twice. No-one had ever given Yorkshire anything in the way of quixotic declarations and in 1971 they were not yet prepared to start doing so. Our bowling was, sadly, not the force it had been. Wilson's decline had started and Geoff Cope was not yet a Ray Illingworth, although we had hopes that he would in time be the right sort of replacement. On paper, the quicker attack of Hutton, Nicholson and the fast-developing Chris Old, was good enough but injury prevented them operating in harness on many occasions. As for the batting, I got 1259 runs but was the only batsman apart from Boycott to top the 1000 mark. All round, we were struggling a bit throughout 1971.

The rift between the senior players was widening all the time and it was not helped by someone's decision – whether it was the captain's or the committee's I don't know – that Sharpe was not a John Player League candidate because of his lack of mobility in the field. I did not subscribe to this because I think Sharpe's mobility was seriously under-estimated, but then very few people had seen him field away from the slips. It was obvious that there was going to be very little call for specialist slippers in the three-ring circus of the

John Player and this is something which people tend to forget
when they piously point to the improvement in outfielding as
a result of one-day competitions. It is equally true that it has
caused a serious decline in the number of specialists in close-
catching positions – slip, short leg and leg slip – and this,
along with the decline in middle-order batting standards, has
caused problems for Test selectors. So Boycott asked me to
open with him in the Sunday games and I was happy enough
to do this because unless you bat between nos. 1 and 4
in the order you are going to have no chance at all to play
a few strokes. This, however, had another disturbing con-
sequence. If Boycott and Wilson both happened to miss a
first-class game through Test calls or injury, Padgett or
Sharpe, as next-senior professionals, became captain. With
Sharpe out of the Sunday games, when Boycott and Wilson
were missing Padgett was the next-senior and therefore took
over the captaincy. So at various times during the season we
had four different captains, all with different ideas, methods,
approaches and attitudes. It didn't help to get together a
settled side with a general policy.

We made a brief flourish in the early part of the season,
before the honeymoon period of harmony with the new
captain was over, and then went rapidly downhill to finish
the County Championship in thirteenth position – the worst
placing this century. For the second successive season we
were knocked out of the Gillette Cup in the first round and in
the John Player we finished next-to-bottom. Closey used to
say, 'Throw down some sawdust, everybody put on top hats
and red noses, and you've got the John Player League.' It
must have seemed a bit like that as we staggered through
the season with just five wins from 16 matches but in that
competition, too, Boycott scored more runs than anyone
else.

There was something wrong somewhere, and it is easy to
see how the pro- and anti-Boycott factions developed. On the

one hand, he was consistently scoring more runs than anyone else; on the other we were losing more matches than ever before. Looked at from the outside it was the easiest thing in the world to say, 'If they all played as well as Geoff, Yorkshire would soon be on top again.' Looked at from within, there was an increasing suspicion in the minds of good and experienced players that they were being relegated to supporting roles for a mega-star virtuoso performance and that the result itself was of secondary importance – a philosophy totally unheard-of in the annals of Yorkshire cricket. The internal mutterings became louder as Boycott, perhaps driven by a growing sense in his own mind of isolation from his senior colleagues, started turning for advice to the scorer, Ted Lester, who had been a good batsman in the post-war decade and then 2nd XI captain when some of us were Colts. Ted had developed into something of a politician and no-one was quite sure what, and how much, he had to say behind the scenes. The rift widened still further.

In the meantime, Boycott himself had become politically involved in one or two directions. First, he offered an apparently harmless opinion about one aspect of the Roses match at Old Trafford which was headlined in the popular Press and Cedric Rhoades, the Lancashire chairman and not one of the greatest Boycott fans, hit back with a prompt rebuke. Then Geoff missed the next game through illness; in fact he did not bat in the second innings of the Roses match, but the Test selectors only found out that he was not well when they telephoned to find out why he had not done so. Their chairman, Alec Bedser, was less than pleased, particularly when he saw, as England followed on against Pakistan at Edgbaston a few days later, that Boycott had recovered enough to lead the county to an innings win over Notts at Headingley – J. H. Hampshire 5 for 37, no less! The storm clouds were gathering all round Boycott. Some were sharply etched against the skyline, like the Cedric Rhoades and Alec

Bedser episodes; others were a little more blurred and built up more gradually, like the unenviable reputation which Geoff had built up of being involved in run-outs.

These stretched back to his earliest days and were fairly generously distributed throughout his career. Personally, I think they have been built up to a disproportionate degree but at the same time, Boycs has been involved in a lot of them, some of them of spectacular dimensions. One of these occurred at Scarborough on 14 July in that unhappy 1971 season with Sharpe, cruelly sent back when hopelessly committed, as the victim. Hutton and Co. were righteously furious on Sharpe's behalf and the mild-mannered PJ expressed himself almost vehemently. Certainly a number of Boycott run-outs were spectacular, involving a pretty obvious indication of disapproval from his partner. These dated back to his earliest days in the side and one which gave Ken Taylor grave affront, at Chesterfield, had led to a mild but official reprimand to Boycott from the captain. Geoff also seriously offended the quiet and undemonstrative Padgett by a twice-in-one-weekend accomplishment at Old Trafford. I did not have very many problems in this respect. Geoff once ran me out very, very badly at Bramall Lane – and in a Roses match when everything has an enhanced significance – and once I left without receiving a ball at Scarborough. The day after the Bramall Lane incident I had a word with Geoff, made my point quite clearly, and he apologised. That was that. As for Scarborough, well, that sort of thing can always happen in a John Player League match and it was something I was not going to get excited about. Then again, I had twice run out Geoff, and one has to consider that in the course of a couple of pretty long careers this sort of thing is bound to happen. But some whose careers were not quite so long, and who felt less philosophical about run-outs, began to dwell on their personal misfortunes; whenever a run-out occurred, it was apt to cause such people to begin recalling experiences of their own.

Finally, in this season of supreme personal success amidst acute and increasing dressing room disharmony, came the celebrated game against Northants at Harrogate. Much criticism has been levelled at Boycott for consciously and deliberately playing for a not out hundred there to ensure his place in the record books as one of the immortals who completed a season with an average of better than 100, and then declaring soon afterwards. I do not subscribe to that criticism and I have to say that if I were in that position, with such a record as the prize, I would be more than a little tempted to go for it myself. In any case, Yorkshire won by an innings and 99 by teatime on the second day, so I cannot see that game as giving too much ammunition to Boycott's critics. At the end of 1971 I was by no means disposed to become a member of the anti-Boycott brigade. He wasn't, to be perfectly frank about it, my sort of bloke, but that was nothing to hold against him. Perhaps I am naive; certainly I have a non-devious way of thinking, so I could not bring myself to believe that Geoff was wholly concerned with personal achievements at the expense of the team performance.

We had started 1971 on a high note and we ended it in mid-September on a high one, too. But that win over Northants was only our fourth of the season and there was no disguising that thirteenth position in the Championship table. Boycott was already a controversial figure in every area; the side was torn apart; there was an obvious feeling amongst some sections of the committee that they had made a mistake. The immediate future did not look too healthy.

12
The Loner

At the end of 1971 Duggie Padgett retired from the game and became the county's coach and 2nd XI captain. I was especially sorry to see Padgett go because in my mind he was the rightful heir to Close's throne as captain. I believe that if he had been made captain, Duggie would have stayed. In the state of unease brought about by that dismal 1971 season, Richard Hutton's name began to be mentioned with increasing frequency as an alternative captain. It was not a campaign which got any sort of support from me. If one put back the clock of one's thinking on the 'right type' to be a county captain, then Richard no doubt had the right sort of social background. There, in my view, his qualifications ended. Warwickshire had started the ball rolling when they made Tom Dollery their captain; the distinction between amateurs and professionals had long since been discarded, and although Yorkshire had been relatively slow off the mark in appointing a real professional as captain (Vic Wilson in 1960), there seemed no logical case to be made out for a return to the 'Corinthian' approach to leadership. Those members of the committee who now had doubts about the wisdom of Boycott's appointment were clearly going to be reluctant to admit that they had made a mistake, and even if they found the courage to change the captaincy it was going to look very bad indeed to those members who were quite simply dazzled by Geoff's run-scoring feats in the otherwise disastrous season which had so recently ended. If the cause of

Yorkshire's misfortunes was Geoffrey Boycott – and personally I was far from convinced that it was – then it was going to be very difficult to do anything about it just yet.

Notwithstanding all these doubts and fears, 1972 started well and we had good wins over Gloucestershire and Glamorgan, honourable draws in rain-affected games against Somerset and Lancashire. We qualified for the knock-out stage of the new Benson and Hedges Cup and in early June we were sitting atop the County Championship table. It was something like the old days, this atmosphere of heady success. It didn't last long.

A crop of injuries and some individual loss of form plunged us into a disastrous June and first Sharpe, then Wilson, lost his place. Rumblings were now becoming ever-louder on the poor record of batting bonus points achieved by Yorkshire in the Championship. With Wilson, the vice-captain, dropped along with Sharpe, now the next-senior player to Boycott, there was a desperate scratching around for a captain when Boycott was absent through injury (he had had a finger broken against Warwickshire in the Gillette Cup) or on Test duty. At one stage Tony Nicholson was called upon to lead the side and once again we heard the name of Hutton being stage-whispered around the grounds. I have no reason at all to believe that the two matters were connected, but about this time Hutton had organised a letter which was to be sent to the committee expressing a lack of confidence in the captain. Initially I agreed to sign it, because clearly all was not well in the camp, but on reflection I decided that I did not feel strongly enough to join in a formal complaint about the captaincy. At that stage I honestly could not see that it was right to hold Boycott responsible for all the problems that we were having, though I accepted that his normal pace of run-scoring was not unconnected with our failure to get as many bonus points as we would have liked. It can certainly be argued that his figures provide full

justification for his methods, but if I have a criticism of Geoff
as a batsman, then it is no more and no less than just about
everyone who has ever batted with him will have felt: he has
left unpunished in his time an awful lot of bad balls. In the
last 20 years Geoff has played so many innings with such an
immense turnover of partners, opening and otherwise, that
first-class cricket is generously populated with players who
have spent a long time observing his technique. It is an
interesting, and in many ways rewarding, experience but I
think all those partners would agree that a lot of bowlers get
away with a lot of half-volleys when they are bowling to
G. Boycott. But this in itself did not seem to me a good and
sufficient reason for joining in a formal condemnation of him
to the Committee, so in the end I refused to sign the letter.

That seemed to put a stop to the letter altogether and I
suppose I was then not entirely popular with the anti-Boycott
faction, but I am not a believer in 'player power'. Without
being in any way pious about it, I can say that I have never
been a devious type of person and really I wasn't very
interested in that sort of behind-the-scenes activity. At the
end of the season we had 'improved' (any Yorkshireman has
to say it with a hollow laugh) from thirteenth to tenth in the
County Championship, but we had reached the first Benson
and Hedges Final, to be beaten by Ray Illingworth's
Leicestershire, and finished joint-third in the John Player
League. It wasn't all a tale of woe. I had also got back into the
England side for two of the one-day internationals and for the
final Test against Australia at the Oval in August. It was a
game worth remembering, not so much for my 42 and 20
runs as seeing Dennis Lillee take three wickets in four balls
for the second time in the series and the Chappell brothers,
Ian and Greg, each score a century in the first innings,
batting together for most of the time. It's always nice to be
involved in a little bit of history in the making, even if you are
on the receiving end.

I even made a personal effort to achieve a bit more harmony in the Yorkshire camp by having a very personal, man-to-man, discussion with Geoff on the subject of the time it took him to make his runs. There had once again been a little dissension in the ranks and after a discussion amongst the other players, in the bar at the end of a game at Hull, I said, 'All right, let's try to get it sorted out.' So I went to see Geoff and told him of the general feeling that, in spite of all the runs he was scoring, the pace at which he did so was not always in the best interests of the side. There was nothing heated about our talk and no tempers were lost. It was, I think, a straight talk between two players of experience and a certain amount of mutual respect. I hoped it had achieved something.

Meanwhile Geoff was doing a good deal of talking in public about changes and reforms he felt were necessary, and some of the subjects on which he offered opinions were quite a distance away from the sort of topics one normally expected to hear from Yorkshire's captain. For instance, he wanted Yorkshire to have their own county ground instead of hiring the club grounds on which they play. This got him into trouble with some civic heads of towns which might, under his scheme, lose their county match. Boycott was also critical of standards in some of the Leagues to which Yorkshire looked for young players. Such views did not endear him any more to his critics on the Committee. Yet as long as he continued to score heavily for Yorkshire and England, the admiration of his personal fan club was increasing to the point of idolatry. As a result, the county club, the members, the players, were drifting into separate camps and the image of Yorkshire's captain as a man you either loved or hated was becoming more sharply defined. If the England selectors had chosen Boycott as captain for the winter tour to India, Pakistan and Sri Lanka in 1972–73 it might well have had a profound effect upon his career from that point. He very badly wanted to lead England and his frustrations in this context brought about an increasing irritation in him as the years went by, leading to more conflict and controversy. I think he certainly should have been given the honour that winter. Ray Illingworth had decided not to go on tour and for me the obvious choice was Boycott on all conceivable grounds. Instead, Tony Lewis was chosen and it has to be recorded that he did a good job in a way Geoffrey Boycott could never have done; ten years afterwards the high regard and affection which the cricketing public of India retained for Lewis indicated all too clearly just what a splendid job he had made of his public relations on the 1972–73 tour. It is not being unfair to Boycott to say that even his most devoted supporter would not have expected that of him. Nevertheless, reverting to a captain of Lewis' amateur-like background because Illingworth was not available must have seemed to Boycott a personal slight and some sort of indication that the selectors were determined that he would not captain England. For the following season, Illingworth was restored to the captaincy after an abortive and pointless Test trial with Illy and Lewis as the rival captains. As Raymond has pointed out, this encounter was fair to neither of them and achieved nothing, but at least with Illingworth as captain again, there could now be no complaint from Boycott that he had a prior claim.

The year 1973 brought the death of the Yorkshire President, Sir William Worsley, thus sadly creating a clean sweep of officials in a very short space of time, since Jack Nash had retired as secretary at the end of the 1971 season. Sir William was a fair and kindly man. We had not only liked him as a President but had appreciated occasional visits, usually for benefit or charity matches, to Hovingham Hall, one of the last bastions of country-house cricket. That year also saw the death of the greatest all-rounder of all time, in terms of figures – Wilfred Rhodes. He was 95 and had been blind for many years and yet it could not quench his enthusiasm for the game of cricket. It was a great experience to sit alongside him at the Scarborough Festival and hear his comments – often caustic – on the subject of field-placing and to share his pleasure in savouring the well-hit stroke which he worked out from the sound of bat on ball.

Arthur Wood also died that year. He was a lovable, whimsical character who kept wicket for England just four times, but one of those occasions was in the Timeless Test of 1938 at the Oval where he described himself as 'just the man for a crisis' as he came to the wicket with England's score reading 770 for 6! Wicket-keepers figure prominently in the ranks of cricket's great characters and Arthur Wood was certainly no exception.

In the County Championship, 1973 was a disappointing season, largely because of our lack of successful spin-bowling. Don Wilson's form seemed to be gradually disappearing and Geoff Cope was struggling in the off-spinner's role because he had had to remodel his action completely after being banned from bowling the previous season. Geoff had done what I considered to be the best thing possible to put things right; he had gone to Johnny Wardle, a left-arm bowler himself but a man with the most immense fund of knowledge and wisdom on all cricketing matters. Cope had emerged with an arm action reminiscent of Johnny himself, coming from behind his back. It passed scrutiny for the time being but Geoff now seemed afraid to spin the ball and while the Test and County Cricket Board finally gave him a clean bill of health as far as the legality of his action was concerned, it seemed that he bothered fewer and fewer bats-men. Yorkshire without an incisive spin attack were like a gun with no bullets. On the other hand, the big-hearted Nicholson had conquered a serious illness and he bowled and bowled and bowled. 'Bluey' Bairstow had made great strides as our wicket-keeper and had won his cap. Sharpe showed better form with the bat and I seemed to have come a little closer to terms with John Player League cricket when I finished the season with a record aggregate of 668 runs. I also had to skipper the side in a number of those Sunday games so there was a certain amount of satisfaction for me when we finished in second place. Chris Old was developing well as an opening bowler and Richard Lumb was coming along as an opening bat. But Barrie Leadbeater, with just about the most flawless technique and style that most of us had ever seen, was now in his fourth year as a capped player and couldn't get a run; there were no Colts knocking clamorously on the door and when injury or Test calls took out any of the established players, quite frequently we were struggling.

We could not, however, blame injuries or Test calls for the disaster which struck Yorkshire cricket at St George's Road, Harrogate, on 30 June 1973. We were bowled out for 135 by Durham, a Minor Counties side, and lost by five wickets, the first time a first-class county had been beaten by a minor county. We finished in fourteenth position in the County Championship – another unwanted record low – and some of our problems were beginning to look insoluble. With Wilson dropped after taking only six wickets at the rate of one every ten overs we tried two young slow left-armers, Phil Carrick from the Bradford League and Mike Bore from Hull. Perhaps more than any other type of bowler, the slow left-armer needs time to learn his trade, to learn to bowl with subtlety and variation, and suddenly there was no time for them to learn. They had to bowl, inexperienced or not, and hard as they both tried, their wickets cost too many runs for us to expect to win matches; they could not be expected to produce match-winning performances while still learning how to bowl. The rumblings began again, this time from outside the dressing room. Ronnie Burnet, who had led us out of the wilderness as captain in 1959, now said publicly that he was in favour of a change in captaincy and went on to suggest that Richard Hutton was the man to take over. Hutton again. But Hutton had told the committee the previous season that owing to business commitments he would no longer be available on a full-time basis so it didn't seem to make much sense. Hutton played just ten first-class innings in 1973 and totalled 65 runs; he bowled 127 first-class overs and took nine wickets at more than 46 apiece!

Captaincy at the best of times is very much a full-time job; captaincy of Yorkshire in this era of recurring crisis looked like involving a lot of overtime as well. I went on record as saying, 'The captain has my full support and the support of all of us.' We were to some extent closing the ranks against outside criticism and I defend our right to do so. I still had a lot of respect for Boycott both as a player and an individual. It was his insistence on pursuing his 'loner' existence which made it difficult to achieve a unanimous team spirit. Most of us got on well with each other, a lot of close friendships existed and despite this depressing run of results it was still possible to feel that one's enjoyment of the cricketing life was not totally impaired. It was a good life, but it would have been a better one if we had all been 100 per cent on the same wavelength. If Geoff had just been able to join in our off-duty relaxations or even the dressing room leg-pulling as one of us, then it would have gone a long, long way towards easing the tensions which crept into our lives when things were going wrong (as they so frequently were now) or when the sniping started from outside our immediate ranks. But he couldn't. He was completely absorbed in his cricket during every waking moment. He could never, it seemed, relax for a minute and somehow he couldn't really talk to any of us except on his own terms.

But if Geoff was in a degree responsible for the way things were continually going wrong, it was difficult to blame him as much as the people who had put him into a position for which he increasingly seemed to be temperamentally unsuited. I was not ready to knock him, or to have him knocked by the very men who had made him captain. So there was a closing of the ranks and – perhaps encouraged by this dressing room support – Geoff gave his views on restoring Yorkshire's greatness in rather far-reaching terms to Ted Dexter in a *Sunday Mirror* article. The wrath of the committee immediately descended on him once again and it was now becoming really difficult to get on with the job of playing good cricket with public controversy constantly raging over and around our heads. It felt a bit like being a member of a ship's crew when the captain is trying to steer one course and the owners want him to go in a completely different direction. Playing cricket for Yorkshire in the 'sixties had been so often a joy and a delight; in the 'seventies it was developing into a nightmare.

It is undoubtedly true that some of the younger players were frightened of Geoff – not in the physical sense, of course, but they were in awe of him as a player and they feared his words and his attitude if they failed to live up to standards he felt they ought to achieve. At the same time he left no-one in any doubt that he regarded himself as the Greatest, a sort of Mohammed Ali complex, and on paper there was not much of an argument anyone could put up about that. And yet, for all his undoubted greatness as a scorer of runs, very rarely did he completely dominate an attack in a way which would have made it so much easier for younger batsmen coming in later. It always had to be done his way and while this was sometimes the best thing for the side, it was not always so. The allegations of selfishness grew and grew.

The Test which ended Ray Illingworth's term of office as England's captain – the third Test at Lord's – also brought Boycott into conflict with Illy over a last-over-of-the-day dismissal and the rumour flew around the game that this had culminated in blows being struck. Raymond has quashed that story but it gained general currency for a time. When the 1973–74 tour to the West Indies began, England had a new captain but once again it was not Geoffrey Boycott. The new leader was Mike Denness, who retained the job for the next year's home series against India and Pakistan.

Early in 1974 there was controversy about our failure to go for a target of 244 in 147 minutes plus the final 20 overs, set in the traditionally delicate atmosphere of the Roses match. The cricket chairman of the county, John Temple, was the man involved with Geoff on this occasion so once again, it seemed, we were off to a fiery start. But it was Yorkshireman arguing publicly with Yorkshireman. It was madness and we were never going to get out of our difficulties that way.

This was the year of Boycott's benefit but it must rank as one of the unhappiest of his career because it marked the start of a three-year exile from the England side. I am pretty sure that the selectors' refusal to make him captain on the West Indies tour still rankled and it must have hurt a good deal when Mike Denness was confirmed for the first three-Test series of that summer, against India, with Tony Greig as vice-captain. Much worse was to come for all of us because, inevitably it now seemed, controversy stalked Geoff day and night and it affected all of us.

We encountered the Indian tourists right at the beginning of the season and for Chris Old it was a remarkable match – a maiden century in Yorkshire's first innings and match figures of 7 for 88 with the ball. For Boycott it was a different story, for he scored 15 and 14, then in the MCC match against the tourists he managed 12 and 1 and in the first Test, at Old Trafford, he got 10 and 6. Every batsman will know something of what he felt. It would be grim enough for what you might call a bread-and-butter cricketer; for Boycott, dedicated to scoring runs all his life, it must have been hideous. Four of those six dismissals came at the hands of Solkar, a useful all-round cricketer but not really the sort of bowler (left-arm, medium-pace, over-the-wicket) you would expect to dismiss Boycs for 14, 12, 1 and 6. This gave rise to a considerable amount of theorising about Geoff's fallibility to a certain form of attack; it was trotted out three years later when Liaqat Ali, a similar type of bowler but a Pakistani, removed him at the start of the 1977–78 tour but that didn't matter over-much. Those early-season dismissals in 1974 did. Geoff seemed to be in a bemused state of mind. It is possible that some of us could have helped if he had felt like letting his hair down and talking to those who had known him for a long, long time. We were all professionals; we had all experienced bad trots; we had all needed a shoulder to cry on at one stage or another of our careers. I feel sure we could have helped to some extent.

Instead, Geoff telephoned Alec Bedser, chairman of the selectors. It was a call which had far-reaching consequences. 'Probably neither of the principals is any longer sure of the exact words,' writes John Callaghan, Boycott's biographer, 'but events ran away with Boycott, who started out in search of understanding and finished up with a rest he was not sure he wanted.' He was not selected for the second Test against India, or the third. He was not picked for any of the three against Pakistan as David Lloyd and Dennis Amiss hit form. Now this could possibly have been the finish of Boycott as a Test batsman altogether, and his captaincy of the county could have suffered severely. Instead, the opposite happened and he made a conscious and obvious effort to get closer to the other members of the team. He let his hair grow a bit longer and took to wearing discreetly flared flannels. He 'got with it.' He became the better half of Jekyll and Hyde, a good companion to go out with, and genuinely made a great effort to change his personality. It is a measure of how depressed and cynical we had become that we still asked ourselves, 'Can the leopard really change his spots?'

A bit of a row developed in mid-season in the form of 'a

difference of opinion over matters of organisation' with Geoff's benefit organiser, Roy Parsons. The next major rumpus came at the end of the season when Tony Greig, who had been made vice-captain of England (like the appointment of Denness, over the head of Boycott), was deposed in favour of John Edrich for that winter's tour of Australia. Again, Boycott had been passed over. What went through his mind when he heard that bit of news, I have no idea, but it is possible to hazard a shrewd guess. He did not go to Australia at all; in fact he did not play for England again until July 1977, when he returned to Test cricket at Trent Bridge, ran out Derek Randall before his own crowd, scored a century and saw the first Test appearance of a man who was destined to become one of the most dynamic characters in English cricket, Ian Botham.

But meanwhile the second Yorkshire honeymoon continued and I must have begun to enjoy my cricket more because my 157 not out against Notts was my first hundred for two years and I followed it with 158 against Gloucestershire and averaged 53 for the season. Richard Lumb had started hitting hundreds and won his cap, Geoff Cope took 77 wickets with (or despite) his new action and even the enigmatic Leadbeater, if he still couldn't contrive a maiden century, managed to give us all a slightly embarrassed laugh by ending on 99 not out in the hundredth over of an innings against Kent. Typical Ledders! Taken all round, the game looked a bit better by the end of 1974. We were beginning to gain a lot of enthusiasm and lost zest, and I couldn't help feeling that if 'the man' had been able to relax to this extent a lot earlier than he did, we might now be well on the way to building up a real rapport between captain and players. We would all have spent a happier three years and probably would have been a lot more successful.

Wilson, Sharpe and Hutton left the county at the end of the 1974 season.

13

False Dawn

The honeymoon continued in 1975. Boycott was making a real effort to get genuinely involved with the team off the field and with their families as well. He encouraged players' wives to come to matches and tried to get rooms set aside for them when they were there. He was more outgoing in every way instead of appearing to be totally withdrawn within himself, and results began to get a lot better. The younger players had had no real chance to develop gradually alongside senior men as I had done and Boycott himself had done, too, but it was to them that we had to turn to replace the experience we had lost.

The most notable of them was Chris Old, who had first played under Brian Close and was now being hailed as the new Trueman. One has to laugh a bit at that because to succeed to such a title would have been difficult in the extreme for a quiet lad from middle-class suburbia in Middlesbrough. But at least he looked quick, was able to manoeuvre the ball and in every way seemed a damned good cricketer. He could bat well at the beginning; later he exhibited the physical distaste for quick bowling which we all have, but which he failed to hide as well as some of us have been able to do. Nevertheless, you cannot take away from him that he developed into an excellent cricketer and as good a practitioner with the new ball as we saw in his time. When he was past his pomp, so to speak, he traded all-out speed for accuracy and guile and again became a supreme player in

that field. I was lucky enough to go to the 1977 Centenary
Test in Melbourne and saw him bowl quite superbly there.
I have been told of his immensely long spells into the wind at
Wellington the following year: 30–11–54–6 in a real snorter
of a gale coming down the Hutt Valley. Many judges rate that
one of Chris's really great performances and I can honestly
say that he gave me everything in my two years as captain.
There were occasions when he missed Test matches because
of injury yet, because we were absolutely hamstrung by our
own casualty list, he turned out with quite serious injury
problems to help out and never once let the side down.

Geoff Cope was the man who had to take over from Ray
Illingworth, so he had a problem similar to Chris Old's.
There has probably never been a more genial or better-liked
player ever to come into the dressing room than Cope, and he
absolutely loved playing cricket. This was infectious and
made him popular amongst a very wide section of our following. It always seemed to me that if there were 20,000 watching us, 19,500 were personal friends of G. Cope. Sadly, his
action was reported as illegal on three different occasions
over eight years, and the last time finished him for good. In
total honesty I have to say that most of us in the side thought
there was something slightly imperfect about his action, yet
at the same time I don't think one could genuinely say that he
chucked it. It was very much a borderline thing and Geoff
struggled with his problem year after year, trying so hard to
get it right.

It's a measure of how close a thing it was that in between
being reported by captains and umpires for delivering the
ball illegally, Geoff was picked for the 1976–77 tour of India
and the 1977–78 trip to Pakistan and New Zealand. On that
second tour he made his Test debut in Lahore and after
toiling away for 38 overs for figures of 0 for 101 he suddenly
took two wickets in two balls. With fielders clustered all
around Iqbal Qasim's bat, the ball was edged into the slips

and on an almost unanimous appeal, the umpire's finger went up. Geoff was in transports of delight, as anyone would have been over a hat-trick in his first Test. For a moment he didn't see that Mike Brearley was indicating to the umpire that he had not in fact made a clean catch in diving for the ball and the batsman, already on his way back to the pavilion, was recalled. In some ways that just about summed up Geoff Cope's career – so near, and yet so far away.

While his action brought no complaint in Pakistan, it did cause remark in New Zealand, particularly in the game against Central Districts at New Plymouth. Districts included a slow left-armer called O'Sullivan who played for a time with Hampshire in the County Championship and whose action really was distinctly suspect. During the game at that most beautiful of grounds at New Plymouth, a friend of mine was asked by a New Zealander what he thought of Cope's action. 'Cope?' he echoed in feigned bewilderment. 'I really couldn't say. I've been too busy watching O'Sullivan.' The New Zealander looked at him thoughtfully for a moment, then remarked, 'Sir, you are a diplomat.'

In Boycott's last year as captain, then again in my first year, Cope was reported again for chucking and by this time Ray Illingworth had arrived as manager. Raymond asked for the help of a television company and they came up to film Geoff bowling under very strict conditions of actual play. Then we went down to their studios in Leeds and viewed the film. It was only when we watched it frame by frame in the slowest possible motion that any imperfection could be noticed, so how opposing captains and some umpires had detected anything wrong, I don't know. Looking around some of the bowlers today, especially some of the quicks, I reckon Geoff Cope got a very raw deal. If there was anything legally wrong (and I am not fully convinced there was), then it was very much a borderline case and Geoff was never going to put anyone in physical danger. There are at least a couple

of very fast bowlers indeed playing in the County Championship today who put everyone in physical danger and whose
actions are very much more obviously questionable than
Geoff Cope's.

The upshot of all Geoff's problems was that he could never
really settle down to bowl as well as he was capable of bowling
and Phil Carrick, learning the trade of the slow left-armer at
the other end, never had the right sort of support to enable
him to develop as we wanted. This, plus the special requirements of one-day cricket, retarded the progress of Carrick
immensely. He was never able to blossom into the imagina-
tive and inventive bowler that Yorkshire's slow left-armer
has always been. Fortunately for Yorkshire he did develop
his batting! But what does intrigue me is that Geoff Cope,
though officially banned from playing first-class cricket, now
plays Minor Counties and Bradford League cricket without
any apparent objection to his action. He loves his game so
much that to be hounded out of all cricket would be the
ultimate crushing blow to Geoff and I would hate to see it.
But how do you get away from the fact that his action is
officially decreed to be illegal at the top level and yet lower
down the professional scale it is apparently all right? Something is very wrong somewhere.

Some of the other youngsters who came through but never
quite measured up to all the requirements of the time were
Peter Squires, Andrew Dalton, Colin Johnson and John
Woodford. I was frankly surprised when Squires was released but it was said that he had a rather nervous disposition
and couldn't conquer the jitters. Well, anyone who has ever
seen him get the ball 25 yards out in a rugby International
and battle his way to the line would obviously doubt that, and
as a fielder he was magnificent.

Andrew Dalton had had an outstanding schoolboy record
and I thought he was a good player, especially after seeing
him save us from a pretty certain defeat by Worcestershire

at Dudley in 1971. There was a feeling in our ranks that
he hadn't (to use a more recent phrase) 'got a lot o' bottle',
but I wish the critics who took that view had seen him play
at Dudley. He had 'bottle' all right. Equally, he had a
self-confidence way beyond his years and his experience,
to such an extent that he became known in the team as 'the
man born to be king'. After being bowled out twice at the
Oval by Pat Pocock on a wet pitch on which it was hardly
possible to compete, we went to Lord's for an extra session
in the nets. As we got there, Prince Edward and some
other young Royals were already at practice and we pointed
this out to Dalton with the comment, 'Now he *was* born
to be king!' Andrew was a good player but he appreciated
his own qualities perhaps a little too ostentatiously.
Inevitably it was an attitude which didn't go down too
well with Boycott, or with one or two members of the
committee either, and he drifted out of the first-class game
after three years.

John Woodford was quite simply the best all-rounder
never to become firmly established in the county game.
Perhaps he was not quite quick enough as a bowler, not quite
good enough with his batting, to add up to a genuine county
all-rounder but he never let Yorkshire down when he played
and he was probably as good a League professional as there
has ever been. He played with great distinction in both the
Bradford League and the North Yorkshire/South Durham
League.

Howard Cooper was a good medium-pace seam-bowler
who was highly respected by other counties. He had good
shoulders and was able to hit the deck with the ball quite
hard, but a series of back injuries reduced his potency. If it
hadn't been for this I think he would have had quite a useful
career. Arthur Robinson was a left-arm fast-medium bowler
who got a regular place in the side rather late in life. He
was a hell of a big feller from a village in North Yorkshire

– we used to call him the Brompton Bull – and on his day was
as good a wicket-taker as anyone around.

So one way and another, there was a fair amount of ability
in the side in the mid-seventies and, with a new and better
atmosphere in the camp, 1975 went pretty well. There were
hopes of a genuine and lasting revival when we finished as
runners-up in the County Championship. Cope, in that
season enjoying a period without complaints against his
action, took 69 wickets at 21.86. The benefit of this to his
spinning partner was immediately obvious and Carrick had
79 wickets at 21.17. Boycott got nearly 2000 runs and
Richard Lumb, with the confidence of his Yorkshire cap,
scored over 1500. I had a lot of injury trouble myself in 1975
but I managed to top 1000 from 19 matches. The news was
not all good, however, because we performed very modestly
in the three one-day competitions and after another season
of battle against injury and illness, Tony Nicholson finally
had to call it a day.

The committee's annual report very rarely displays
emotion of any kind but one detects a sort of lump-in-the-
throat note in its passage relating to Nick's enforced retirement: 'Yorkshire never had a more whole-hearted worker for
the good of its cause both on and off the field. "My county,
right or wrong" was essentially his philosophy. He takes with
him into retirement the best wishes and thanks of the whole
Yorkshire cricket public for 13 years achievements (including six championships) during that period.' That is
stirring stuff indeed in the context of an annual report and
no-one deserved it more than Nick. He was a fine bowler, a
great team man, a superb mate. His departure must have had
some significance for Boycott, too, because the three of us
had developed about the same time and come through the
Colts together. In those days before Geoff had got his first
car, Nick had driven him about the country quite a lot, too.
If we were travelling north, then I would pick him up in

Fitzwilliam; if we were going south, it would be Nick's turn, driving down from Dewsbury. Geoff obviously appreciated Nick as a bowler and was going to miss him sorely. He's not a sentimental bloke but I'll bet a good deal that he also knew he was going to miss him as a dressing room character and, quite simply, as a friend from way back. The three of us had come a long way together.

22 May 1976 provided a parallel with our Gillette Cup defeat at the hands of Durham and another unwanted record as we went down to the Combined Universities in the Benson and Hedges Cup at Barnsley, of all places. My schoolboy memories at that particular ground were a little happier! This time I was very much in the firing line because I captained the side in Boycott's absence. He had broken a bone in his hand in the John Player match at Old Trafford and missed nine Championship matches so I was involved in a fair amount of captaincy that season and I can't say it was a conspicuously successful period. But nothing could have been worse than defeat by the University boys, especially in view of the miserable way we slumped to defeat. We made a very slow start because Leadbeater was not by nature a man to force the pace and Athey was very new to our ranks. So much time was used up that a bit of panic set in and I was run out without scoring as I tried in desperation to get things moving. We totalled a wretched 185 for 7 in our 55 overs and I think we must in fairness be said to have underestimated the students. They included men who were later to make a distinct mark in county cricket – Vic Marks, Chris Tavaré, Paul Parker and Peter Roebuck – but we had no excuses. Having batted badly, we bowled badly with Chris Old, normally a model of line and length bowling, spraying short-pitched deliveries all over the place and we were beaten by seven wickets.

Six years later, Peter Roebuck, a brilliant essayist, produced a joyous description of events as seen from the opposition ranks after Leadbeater and Athey had taken 14 overs to score our first 17 runs. Universities' first-change bowler was A. R. Wingfield-Digby, a name not often mentioned on the playing fields of Barnsley, and his introduction brought a buzz of sardonic interest in Arthur Scargill country. 'Wingers-Diggers' later became a parson. 'Digby,' wrote Roebuck, 'does have one enormous advantage over lesser mortals: as a man of the cloth he can summon formidable powers to his assistance. . . . Our Reverend trundles up to bowl his loosener. A shade short (atheists call 'em long hops), it causes Leadbeater to essay a hook to the mid-wicket boundary. He succeeds only in edging it onto his stumps. Well, there you are, you see. . . . Athey falls and acting captain John Hampshire walks in to sort out all this nonsense. A player of quality, John could turn this game in half an hour. He defends his first two balls from Savage, then drives to me at mid-on. Suddenly he charges for a desperate single. I hit the stumps and Hampshire is gone.'

I couldn't have put it better myself – though perhaps with less relish! For the University lads it was an occasion for rejoicing in the highest possible spirits. For us it was the ultimate humiliation. While the 'schoolboys' frolicked exultantly, we locked the dressing room doors and hard words were spoken. Boycott, an injured spectator at the game, took part. The whole of our lack of success, not only in that game or in that season, came under review. In six seasons we had been beaten by a minor county, achieved the lowest Championship placing in 70 years and then gone one worse, and now we had lost in a one-day match to forces much despised by Yorkshiremen of old, 'the coloured caps'. This was rock-bottom and a lot of frank talking took place behind the closed doors of Barnsley's home dressing room. From the press, and the Yorkshire press in particular, I took a lot of stick and that was right. I was the captain and therefore it was my responsibility. I make no excuses for the defeat. We played badly and the 'schoolboys' played well. The team spirit which had begun to burgeon during the honeymoon period was largely dissipated and in some ways we were back to square one. Boycott scored 1288 runs in first-class matches that year and I got 1303. No-one else reached four figures. We dropped from second to eighth in the Championship table, lost to Gloucestershire in the Gillette, finished third-from-bottom in the John Player and made that abject exit from the Benson and Hedges. The fact had to be faced that we were not winning anything because we were not good enough to win.

In July 1977, Boycott returned to the England fold, scoring 107 and 80 not out at Trent Bridge. At the time of his selection Yorkshire were the only unbeaten side in the Championship but straightaway it was as if Geoff had become totally absorbed in playing Test cricket again and that everything else was of lesser significance. When he came back from, admittedly, a magnificent Test at Trent Bridge, the conversation was now all about Test cricket, money, records and the England captaincy. The more pressing matters at hand seemed to have no real place in his thoughts. The England captaincy did, and it must have been yet another severe blow to Boycott when Greig – deposed for his part in organising the Packer 'Circus' – was replaced by Mike Brearley, who was then appointed to lead the winter tour to Pakistan and New Zealand. But first came another milestone in a Boycott career which was paved with them. My collaborator in this book, partly out of respect for Geoff's batting ability, partly from his knowledge of Geoff's great sense of occasion, forecast in a Radio 2 cricket commentary on Saturday 6 August that Boycott would complete the ninety-ninth first-class century of his career at Edgbaston on Monday 8 August and go on to reach the hundredth hundred in the fourth Test at Headingley starting the following Thursday. Absolutely on cue Boycott did just that, emphasising that no-one can ever knock his tremendous achievements as a scorer of runs in very large quantities. His feats have been quite prodigious and that particular one was marked by a historic photograph being taken of three generations of great Yorkshire opening batsmen together – Herbert Sutcliffe, Sir Leonard Hutton and Geoffrey Boycott. It's a marvellous picture for cricket historians to treasure but it is ironical to look at those three smiling faces and reflect that Hutton has often and severely criticised Boycott's attitude to the game while the late Herbert Sutcliffe wasn't very keen on him as an individual.

In uncannily exact ratio, dressing room relationships now deteriorated as Boycott's personal career took off once again. He went off on tour as vice-captain of the England party, perhaps with hopes that now he would be regarded as the logical successor to Brearley in due course. That came earlier than expected because Brearley suffered a broken forearm in a quite meaningless one-day game in Karachi and flew home, leaving Boycott as captain for the final Test in Pakistan (an abortive draw as the previous two had been) and three in New Zealand. There it fell to his unfortunate lot to lead the first England team ever to be beaten by New Zealand in a Test, although I am categorically assured that there was nothing he could have done to prevent it, so badly did the rest of the side bat and so magnificent was Richard Hadlee's bowling. But some ugly rumours about the team's dissatisfaction with his captaincy have come out of the second Test, in Christchurch, in spite of the fact that it was won to square the series. Rightly or wrongly, misunderstood or not, unfairly condemned or not, Boycott was not appointed captain or even vice-captain for the next tour. By then, though, more drama had been witnessed on the Yorkshire stage.

The rumblings from the committee room about our continued lack of success, and the reasons for it, had grown to

a major explosion in September 1977 when Don Brennan,
the former wicket-keeper, called publicly for the removal of
Boycott as captain and nominated Geoff Cope as the replacement. This immediately brought the formation of a Reform
Group, and the circumstances of its birth cannot really make
it anything other than a Boycott Supporters' Club. At that
time there was nothing really wrong with that; if a group of
members felt strongly enough about threats to a man they
fervently admired, they were entitled to their view and to
their vociferous support of that man. It was later that their
operations assumed a more sinister aspect with results
which, in my view, were even more disastrous for Yorkshire
County Cricket Club. I didn't know it at the time but the formation of that Reform Group was the beginning of the end
for me.

14

Poles Apart

There was still nothing radically untoward about the relationship between Geoff and myself in 1978. We had drifted apart in the social sense from the relatively close contacts that had been established during his absence from the England side, but we could still talk cricket on an intelligent and reasonably cordial level. At the same time he was engaged in a sort of running battle with one or more members of the committee at various times. Geoff had a lot of strong views on what he thought should be done in various organisational and administrative areas and gradually, I think, the feeling grew that he was trying to become an altogether too powerful figure. As the chorus from the Reform Group increased in volume, the greater grew what seemed to be quite clearly a power struggle. I tried to close my eyes and ears to it. It wasn't at all the sort of way I expected Yorkshire CCC affairs to be conducted. It was this power struggle, I'm sure, which prompted a sub-committee led by Michael Crawford (then treasurer, now chairman) to approach Ray Illingworth with an offer of the managership of Yorkshire from the start of the 1979 season – the first appointment of that kind there had ever been. The negotiations were kept a close secret and even the county committee didn't know about them until the appointment was fixed up, but it leaked out into the Press early in 1978. Naturally enough, Boycott was concerned about the exact areas in which he and the manager would exercise control, but we were all interested in one way or another. Geoff and I talked it over during a Sunday League match against Glamorgan, and we arranged to have dinner with Ray when we played against Leicestershire in June 1978 to discuss his views on the management of the county. But Boycott did not play in the game at Grace Road and I went alone to see Ray. During the meal, one of the issues raised was that Geoff had previously said to Ray that he didn't trust me.

I went straight up the wall.

For seven years I had refused to take sides against him, no matter who invited or pressed me to do so. I had refused to sign a letter of no confidence in him to the committee. I had always tried to find something to be said in his favour when discussions critical of the captain were taking place. I had refused to join any anti-Boycott faction and, while it had never been possible for us to become close friends, I had always tried to discuss things with him soberly and sensibly. On the occasion six years before in Hull when I had had my chat with him it was to try to prevent an open breach being created between him and some of the more experienced members of the side. And now I learned that he had obviously told other people he did not trust me, for it to get back to Illy.

At the first opportunity I sought out Boycott and gave him a chance to put his side of the story. When he didn't give me a satisfactory answer I was livid. To be told that I was untrustworthy represented a vicious insult to me and I was not going to stand for it. I told him exactly what I thought of him and reported the matter to the chairman. A little later, when both Leicestershire and ourselves were without a match, the three of us – Boycott, Illingworth and myself – were asked to see the chairman, Arthur Connell, separately. This seemed to clear the air but my attitude to Boycott was now changed. He was a man who had cast doubts on my trustworthiness and he had done it behind my back. From now on I looked at everything he did in a different light. Then, on 17 July, came the famous Northampton go-slow.

Boycott had scored 50 in over three hours and his hundred took more than 4½ hours against not the greatest attack in the world, while Bill Athey had played a magnificent knock of 114. I passed Bill on the way out to bat, but nothing was said and Boycott was still grinding away at the other end. The field was set back and scoring wasn't easy, but I hadn't been there for 4½ hours or more. All the same, I had not gone in with any idea in my mind other than playing the way I had always done. No thought of any sort of protest or demonstration had occurred to me. But when Geoff finally went for 113 in getting on for five hours I suddenly thought, 'What the hell's it all about? We've watched slow batting for so long. Now I'm going to see what it's like.' Call it a brainstorm if you like, but towards the end of that innings I just decided I was going to play the way we had seen Boycott play so many times. The Northants players sensed there was something odd going on and started to laugh a bit. I had a word with Colin Johnson, the new batsman, and told him, 'Don't worry. If there are any repercussions, I'll take responsibility.' And we scored 11 runs from the last ten overs.

To this day I am unsure what exactly prompted my gesture but I do remember thinking to myself, 'Why should it have to be somebody else who plays all the strokes and chases for bonus points? I'm going to pat a few back myself, or offer no stroke, or decline a good single. Let's just see what it's like.'

When the innings ended the dressing room had cleared. There are two rooms at Northampton and the outer one was empty. I had changed in the back room with Boycott and one or two others but now he was the only occupant. He was sitting with his head in his hands and I expected something to be said. Nothing was said – not a word. Ten minutes later

121

we went out to field. The Yorkshire president, Sir Kenneth Parkinson, was there, as was Billy Sutcliffe, a committee-man, and they could have come in and given me a bollocking if they felt like it, but they didn't. Next day I was absolutely flabbergasted at the reaction in the press. I didn't think my gesture, if you want to call it that, merited the near-hysteria which showed the following morning. I was annoyed, too, that Boycott didn't say anything to me, man to man, but left it to the committee. It was from the press that I learned that I was to be asked for an explanation by the committee, and this took place on the afternoon and evening of the first day of a rain-affected Gillette Cup game at Bradford immediately after we had come home from Northampton. It all seemed to me to have been ridiculously magnified: there I was, standing at one end of the Bradford bar talking things over with a group of friends, Boycott at the other end surrounded by his newspaper friends, and Joe Lister, the Yorkshire secretary, popping out from the committee room to call us in in turn.

When my turn came I walked in and, before anyone else spoke, I asked, 'Well, are you sacking me, or what?'

The reply was, 'Oh no, John. Nothing like that.' What they did say, which made sense, was that if I had wanted to make a protest I should have gone for the one remaining bonus point available and then made my view known after-wards, off the field.

I accept that, but at the same time I don't regret what I did, largely because it was in no way pre-meditated and it must have been prompted by some deep-seated need to react in some obvious way to yet another hour-after-hour grind, with me (and others) then being required to go and show the flashing blade. Perhaps it was the one straw required to break this particular camel's back. I do know that it was not planned in any way and it was not discussed with anyone. It was simply a reaction to circumstances I had come to know only too well.

Contrary to what I had expected, there was no hostility in that committee room. They were not exactly friendly and they pointed out my error in making the protest in the way I had done, but there was no bollocking or anything resembling one. Consequently I was staggered next day to learn from newspaper stories that I had been 'reprimanded and warned as to my future conduct'. That was totally untrue; nothing of the nature had been said at all. The committee in fact told me that they appreciated that Boycott's slow scoring had been going on for a long time and that it sometimes put other batsmen under pressure, but that I shouldn't have made my protest in the way I did. That was it, and I accepted it.

So when the press stories appeared I contacted the cricket committee chairman, John Temple, and told him, 'You didn't say anything to me about reprimands and warnings.'

He replied, 'No, but it seems as though Boycott has issued his own press statement.'

So what did happen after that meeting? One national newspaperman recalls it vividly, he tells me, and this is his version of what occurred: 'I remember waiting into the hours of darkness outside the first-floor room at Park Avenue until the "trial" was over. John Temple tried to dismiss the whole thing as "purely an internal matter". Then, pressed for a statement, he said, "I haven't time to answer questions; my wife is cooking my dinner." Hampshire refused to comment. Boycott hung around at the back of the room inviting – or so I thought – questions. It turned into a muttered press conference between the captain and those members of the press he thought he could trust. Nothing was quotable but I came away with the impression that the committee had backed him and bollocked Jake. As I recall, other papers shared that view. Subsequent events suggest that we all grabbed the wrong end of the stick which was proffered to us. I am not sure who should take the blame, but Yorkshire must share it for refusing to confirm or deny the only source of information open to us.'

After a lot of lessons in this sort of situation, Yorkshire still had to learn that newspapers, if denied official information, will still get their stories from some other source; this is just one more example of how misleading and unfortunate they can be at times. Yet the story the papers all missed, and which only came to light four years later (in fact when I started to produce this book), throws some remarkable light on the administrative in-fighting of the late 'seventies and indicates to what extent the camp was divided. It also helps to explain the lack of official information. The sub-committee which conducted that hearing at Park Avenue drew up a statement to be issued which was critical of Boycott and made particular reference to his 'selfish batting'. Before it could be made public, the contents of the statement were brought to the notice of the club president, Sir Kenneth Parkinson, who promptly quashed it, saying, 'You cannot criticise the captain in that way'. It was not until the next committee meeting, when men like Don Brennan and Ronnie Burnet asked what had happened to the statement, that they learned of Sir Kenneth's intervention, and they were furious. The president is really a figurehead with no executive status, although in real terms he is usually someone whose stature is such that he can wield definite influence. There is no doubt that Sir Kenneth Parkinson used his influence on Boycott's behalf on more than one occasion.

While all this was going on, Judy had been ill for some time with a gall bladder complaint. She was due to go into hospital that afternoon for major surgery the following day. She had to drive herself to hospital and was admitted on her own. As the 'trial' went on later and later, I had to ask Steve Oldham (the fast bowler who is now a team-mate at Derbyshire) to wait for me and take me to hospital to see Judy and pick up my car. I had to carry on playing cricket for Yorkshire.

Boycott has certainly had his share of playing under all sorts of outside pressures, but those Reform Group members who were to make my life (and the lives of my family) a misery over the next two or three years should be aware that he is not unique in having to experience such pressures.

That meeting at Park Avenue took place in July. From then on things were rather tense, and the worst of it was that the dressing room was divided into players who supported Boycott, players who supported me and others who supported neither camp. It was an unhealthy and unhappy state of affairs and by the end of the season I had decided to leave Yorkshire. After the Northampton incident, with its obvious implications, Derbyshire had asked me if I was interested in the captaincy, as Eddie Barlow was leaving them at the end of 1978. I had a meeting with the Derbyshire secretary, David Harrison, and listened with interest to their plans for the future. I was indeed interested in joining them, especially in view of the extremely unhappy situation in Yorkshire. There was no way I could see it improving in the forseeable future and even though my whole adult life had been orientated towards Yorkshire cricket, at 37 I wanted to be able to enjoy my remaining years in the game and to be able to put something back into it. This was now looking less than possible in Yorkshire. I saw the club chairman, Arthur Connell, and asked for my release. He said he didn't want me to go and then, somewhat to my surprise, he asked whether I would be able to handle Boycott if I was made captain. I said that that remained to be seen because all kinds of attitudes were involved and there had already been suggestions in newspapers that if Boycott were relieved of the captaincy, he would contest it. Plainly, it was not going to be an easy role if I took it on. So much would depend upon Boycott's attitude and, of course, on how many of the players still supported him. Yet I believed, and still do, that the captaincy of Yorkshire is the highest honour in the game. I had not sought it, but I decided I was not going to turn it down if it was offered.

I told David Harrison perfectly frankly what the position was. If Yorkshire offered me the captaincy, I would take it. If they didn't, I would join Derbyshire, and I left it at that with both counties as I prepared for a winter's playing engagement in Tasmania. The day before I was due to leave, John Temple telephoned me about four in the afternoon and asked whether I would accept the Yorkshire captaincy.

Judy and I were in the middle of packing and I looked at her enquiringly across the room. She gave a little nod. I drew a deep breath and thought to myself, 'By heck, count to ten.' Finally I replied, 'Yes. Fine.'

He said, 'Right, the job's yours.'

I turned to Judy and said, 'There's going to be all sorts of bother here. I'm going out.' I rang up Steve Oldham and said, 'Pick me up, old pal. There's going to be a bit of bother on here.' Judy took the telephone off the hook and told callers at the door that I had gone to watch a football match. So we survived the attention of the press that night and next day flew off to Hawaii for a holiday with Jack Simmons and his family before starting the season in Tasmania. Looking back, if I had known the sort of flak that the appointment was going to cause, I would never have accepted the captaincy, much as I had always regarded it as the greatest honour in the game. I had never asked for it, never honestly wanted it. But so important did the position seem to me, so significant a distinction is the Yorkshire captaincy, that it is not an honour you turn down. I think Ian Botham must have felt something like this when he came back from the 1980–81 tour of the West Indies and carried on as England's captain through a formidable barrage of criticism. He couldn't turn down the captaincy of his country; I couldn't turn down the captaincy of my county. But if I had even dreamed of the incredible distress and unhappiness it was going to cause, I would have turned it down.

Throughout my winter in the Australian summer, Joe Lister kept me up to date with the furore raging around the county club – protests, petitions, comparisons, the Reform Group waging an all-out campaign on Boycott's behalf. We had phone calls from people in England at such ridiculous hours that we had to take the phone off the hook. Increasingly it was becoming obvious that a great deal of ugliness was building up and as Boycott was now on tour with the England party in Australia, our next meeting was getting a great big build-up in the form of advance publicity. This might well have suited the press; possibly it suited Boycott; but it certainly didn't suit me. Life was clearly going to be hard enough the following summer without any widely publicised confrontation during the winter in Australia while the Reform Group were doing their stuff back home. Boycott might have felt – probably had every reason to feel – that he had been wronged, but it was through no effort on my part and I was determined not to be put into an artificially contrived situation as the architect of Boycott's martyrdom.

Eventually the great day dawned when I was to play against the tourists in Hobart. Already some journalists had offered the view that I ought to have been at the airport to greet Boycott, as his new captain. They wouldn't have been wanting an interesting picture, would they? In any event, I was far too pre-occupied when the party arrived, and in fact I missed the game in Launceston because our younger son, Paul, had been hit on the head by a cricket ball during a net practice and he was in hospital very seriously ill indeed for a time. At Hobart I didn't see Boycott before the match started but we sat pretty close to each other at lunch a couple of times without any words being exchanged. On one occasion when rain stopped play I went back to the tourists' hotel and had a few drinks with Jack Simmons, Chris Old and David Bairstow without Boycott appearing.

Finally Terry Brindle, cricket correspondent of the *Yorkshire Post*, asked me, 'Are you going to say anything to Geoff?' I said I was perfectly happy to chat to him if we met, but I wasn't going to look for him simply to do so. Terry said it was my place to seek Geoff out first and I disagreed. Then I went out to dinner with Chris Old and he said, 'You really ought to get together for the good of the side next season' and I agreed. 'But,' I added, 'I'm not going to go cap-in-hand, which seems to be what he wants.'

Now Tasmania had won the Australian Gillette Cup and that involved us in a match against the England side in Melbourne, so off we went on 3 February. It was a blooming awful day and it wasn't a very good game, but while we were all limbering up the previous day and having various forms of practice, Boycott was in one of the England nets so casually I walked over and bowled a few at him, calling, 'Are you all right then?' Geoff replied, 'Yes, thanks. Are you?' And that was it. I had made a conscious effort to break the ice and I think I could be said to have made the first move. Then it was a matter of getting on with the practice. But not so with the press. Several photographers moved in and asked, 'Will you bowl a few more at him?' I replied, 'Certainly not.' I see nothing wrong in that from any standpoint. I was not there for the benefit of newspaper photographers and neither was Boycott. My gesture was a personal one from me to him and it had nothing to do with publicity from any point of view. Certainly I was making a gesture but I was making it in the interests of Yorkshire cricket and my own captaincy of the side – not for anyone else at all. Somewhere along the line someone had to make a move and as far as I was concerned I had made it.

The following day, on the way home after the game, Judy said, 'Chilly [ie. Chris Old] came to see me yesterday and said Boycs will talk to you providing Brindle [Terry Brindle, of the *Yorkshire Post*] can be there.'

My reaction was immediate and entirely spontaneous: 'He must be joking.' I spoke to Chris Old and he confirmed the message and, quite frankly, I said, 'Bollocks.'

Boycott could have come to me at any time for a chat; I had already held out the olive branch. We were presumably hoping to be associated with Yorkshire cricket during the following summer. What on earth had a newspaperman got to do with it and why was a personal meeting between Boycott and myself dependent upon the presence of the *Yorkshire Post's* cricket correspondent? What was Boycott trying to do?

I went home and reported for training the day after I got back. It was quite tense because the team were not sure how I was going to be, how Boycott was going to be or even how Illy was going to be, for he had now taken over as manager. It was fortunate that the first spell was spent at the Carnegie Physical Education College, and if anything was bothering anyone seriously he could sweat it out! We had to put up with the staged pictures of Raymond with Boycs and myself, all with our arms round each others' shoulders and captions reading 'All is forgotten' and that sort of rubbish.

It wasn't going to be easy, that summer of 1979, I realised that. I had written to Ray Illingworth from Australia after seeing just a little of the campaign of vilification which was taking place back home, to say that there was no way I wanted to captain a side which did not support me, so I asked him to arrange some sort of canvass of the team's views. He replied that this had been carried out and I had a large majority of support within the team. Now when I came back I wasn't so much interested in who had been 'for' and who 'against' in that list as hoping that they would all do their damnedest for Yorkshire. I knew that certain players had been pro-Boycott in the past and that was fair enough, especially if a man was on the fringe of England selection and took the view that Boycott could in some way help him reach the Test side. I certainly wasn't going to blame him for that, and such players were, and still are, good friends of mine: there is nothing in my book which says you have to lose a mate's friendship simply because you don't agree with all his views, or he with yours.

During the next two years we may not have performed with great success but I genuinely believe that they all gave me everything they had got. Boycott himself mellowed after a difficult start. For a long time he never spoke or greeted me when I went into the dressing room and he extended this to people he thought had supported me, but I forced him to speak by greeting him first. It wasn't ideal but it was something. While I did not get any help from him in the voluntary sense, if I did approach him, then more often than not he gave me the answer I wanted. It was simply that he would not help of his own volition. Fortunately, with Chris Old on the field and Illy off it, there was help around. Although I was not looking for anyone to make my mind up for me and in the last analysis the captain has to make the decisions, no-one is too big to respect the advice of his colleagues and to weigh up all the points before making a decision. All the same, in that first year I found myself almost frightened to make a decision because I began to feel that about 98 per cent of the crowd were against me and waiting, hoping, for me to make a mistake. That seems a big percentage, I know, but that's how I felt and it got worse in the second year. Yet I couldn't jack it in at the end of the first year after all the strife and controversy which had surrounded my appointment. That would have been letting down the people who had faith in me and, I thought, plunging us into another crisis. But I was not happy and I didn't enjoy my cricket very much at all.

Illy gave me all the support he could and I have no complaints about his attitude, but he did experience difficulty in some disciplinary matters. There was a tendency for the team to take advantage of the great division amongst supporters, and there was a slackening of standards in behaviour and those general matters in which you expect professional cricketers to discipline themselves. Sadly, looking back, I suppose it was understandable. A sort of anarchy was reigning throughout the county's cricket. The manager, the captain, the committee, were being publicly reviled by people professing to have the club's best interests at heart and the players – especially the younger or less mature ones – cannot have helped feeling that there was a lowering of standards all around them. It was all very nasty and it was becoming utterly impossible to concentrate on playing cricket, let alone playing it well.

Raymond and I spent a lot of time together, partly because we are long-standing friends (and our families as well), partly because we were the two people who had to sort things out, but from time to time I became very depressed indeed. Yorkshire's cricket was not going well; the nastiness I now experienced was unbelievable; and, to make it much, much worse, it washed over my family as well – the kids at school, my wife when she went shopping. They were all subjected to snide remarks and clearly defined hostility wherever they went. The Reform Group had done its work well, and how those people can ever stand up and say they have the interests of Yorkshire cricket at heart passes belief. It was as though I had done something terribly wrong, but this I simply cannot accept. I had not sought the captaincy; I had never, over the whole period of his captaincy, agitated for the removal of Boycott. I admit that I had been guilty of one breach of good taste in expressing disagreement with him by my action at Northampton, and I had agreed to sign Richard Hutton's anti-Boycott letter and then changed my mind. But if these were the only blemishes on the escutcheon covering a pretty long career, then I felt it wasn't a bad record. But by halfway through the 1979 season that attitude, almost of hatred, which I felt coming from one section of supporters had driven me to such a point that I didn't want to go out of the house at night. I no longer wanted to visit the haunts which had been regular calling-points after games for so many years. If I did, someone would inevitably slide up and trot out a bit of unpleasantness. It did not all necessarily come from members of the Reform Group themselves – apart from the leaders I am still unaware who the other members are or how many of them exist – but it was very plainly coming from people who had been thoroughly brain-washed by the propaganda which had poured out during my absence during the winter. At no time had I ever had a chance to tell them what I thought or felt or believed. It came from people who believed Boycott should still be captain and I had no objection to that as a viewpoint; I respect loyalty to friends and heroes. I could even understand that they might resent his successor, but I could not for the life of me understand the personal bitterness with which they seemed to hold me responsible for the fact that their man was not captain. It all hurt me very badly and, more important, it hurt my family.

It was a far cry from the life I had known in the 'sixties, from the life I had grown up longing to enter. Occasionally one or two of the lads – Chris Old, Richard Lumb, 'Bluey' Bairstow – would sense my total depression and say, 'Come on, Hamps. We're taking you out for the night,' and for a little while life would take on a brighter hue. But then it was back to the back-biting and bitching and back-stabbing from the people who were supposed to support Yorkshire. I was becoming sick of it all.

The external pressures were so much greater than any-thing from within the dressing room that I felt as though I could not make a move without being hounded, and after two years I had had enough. The majority feeling was that we wanted Richard Lumb as captain for 1981. He would not take it on with Boycott in the side so Chris Old was invited to lead the county and accepted. Off he went to the West Indies with Boycott on the England tour and they came back, apparently, the best of pals. 'Chilly's' view now was: 'He's my senior professional and vice-captain and all the help I want, I'll get from him.' Everything in the garden was lovely.

Or at least, it was until about mid-season when Old and Boycott had a bust-up in which Boycott told Old that if he wanted any advice in future he could get it from somewhere else. We limped through to the end of another sorry season, reeling from one crisis to the next. When Old was injured, Lumb was supposed to be captain. When Lumb was injured as well as Old, what was Illingworth to do with the two immediate ex-captains in the side? He telephoned me one day, when Old and Lumb were injured and said, 'I know you'll think I've gone round t'back o' t'moon but I'm thinking of making Neil Hartley captain.'

I thought about it, then replied, 'Well, you *have* gone round t'back o' t'moon. I don't know whether you're trying to hang yourself or get yourself sacked, but you're wrong.'

That's the only time we have agreed to disagree. I felt that when we had a full side in the field, Hartley would struggle to find a place. And then there was Bairstow, who had skippered in some one-day games and done a good job. Raymond, however, felt it was too hard to keep wicket and captain a side – a view, incidentally, I have since confirmed with Bob Taylor of Derbyshire. Nevertheless, I still pressed for Bairstow and when Illy would not agree I finally said, 'Look, I'll do it until Chilly is fit. I don't want to but it won't seem as bad to Bluey and some of the others as it will if Neil is made captain.'

So I captained Yorkshire in Glamorgan and against Notts and we lost both games handsomely, after which Hartley was captain when Old was not available. It was during the

Glamorgan game that I experienced the sort of mysterious chest pains which caused Fran Cotton to come home from the British Lions tour of South Africa and for a couple of days I was pretty bad. Whether it was the pressure of being back in command I don't know, but it was distinctly unpleasant at the time.

I believe that one or two players made life difficult for Hartley, and Illy was aware of it. His view was quite straightforward: 'I've made the decision and if they don't like it they can leave the club.' So we staggered on punch-drunk, some of us, from defeats, dissension, discord. I never dreamed that it was possible to play cricket in such an atmosphere of unbridled animosity, most of it from the public but some of it from within. Every time I thought things could not get worse, they did. Then we reached 9 September 1981 at Scarborough, where I had spent so many joyful days playing cricket, like hundreds of other cricketers of all other counties and generations. It was here that we hit rock bottom and Yorkshire cricket experienced its blackest moment.

I came down to breakfast in our hotel before the first day's play against Northants and was joined by Illy and Chris Old. Now to set the scene: (1) the Reform Group had started a hue and cry for the sacking of Raymond as manager; (2) Boycott had somehow or other been out of touch with the manager, despite Raymond's efforts to reach him, since playing in the sixth Test against Australia at the Oval the previous week; (3) he had appeared in a television interview and said he 'intended to clear the air' with Illingworth when the season was complete; (4) this had been picked up by the press and there was intense speculation as to what would happen next.

That was the background to the situation that morning as I was joined at the breakfast table by a grim-faced Chris Old. After the usual pleasantries and reading through some of the papers, I asked Old, 'Are you going to drop him, then?' Chris nodded and nothing more was said. Now the reason I asked the question was that that TV interview had placed Boycott, so far as we all knew, in breach of his contract with Yorkshire which prohibited public statements by players on club matters. What we didn't know at that time and, incredibly, *what Illingworth, the manager, had not been told*, was that Boycott had a different contract from the rest of us with that particular clause missing!

I walked down to the ground, as I always have done, from the Royal Hotel and already the ground was buzzing while one or two of the players were walking round in a daze, it seemed. I have always changed next to Boycott in the Scarborough dressing room and I found him changing out of whites back into his suit. 'What's up?' I asked, really for something to say because although I had had the nod from Old at breakfast, it still seemed necessary to say something. 'I've been left out,' Boycott replied. We had had 'atmospheres' in the dressing room many times in the past but nothing like this one. There was a general scampering to get out and practise, even though it was the end of the season and the crowds were pouring into the ground even at that early stage. The Reform Group were extremely prominent amongst the numbers and extremely vocal, too. Never can a county match have started in such an atmosphere. The start was in fact delayed by five minutes because shouting, heckling spectators were milling around on the pitch. I was so tense and nervous when my turn came to bat that I was almost shaking. It was appalling.

Boycott, instead of leaving the ground as I think he should have done, stayed signing autographs, receiving (presumably) the sympathy of his admirers, and generally holding court. Beside him stood Sid Fielden, the Doncaster policeman and leading member of the Reform Group, collecting signatures for the Illingworth-must-go petition. And out in the middle, Yorkshire were trying to play a County Championship match! I was sick to the depths of my

135

soul. Was it for this I had cherished those childhood ambitions, laboured through those years of bus and tram and train journeys to the nets, hoped and prayed for my chance to come to play for this county, taken knocks on the head and blows to the heart? This was the end, the last nail in the coffin of Yorkshire cricket as far as I was concerned. I wanted no more of it.

I went to Derbyshire to see if it was possible once more to find joy and pleasure and laughter in playing cricket.

15

The End – and a New Beginning

After 20 years in one county's dressing room there were inevitably things which were going to be different and the first I noticed was the noise or, in Derbyshire's case, the lack of it. Even in our worst times, Yorkshire's had remained noisy – as it would with, in different generations, men like Wilson, Nicholson, Bairstow, Stevenson in its ranks. Derbyshire's was very much quieter and in many ways it was a pleasant change. Each member of the side received me well in his own individual way, and I was treated with the kindness that an old man was entitled to expect!

So my welcome to Derbyshire was as cordial as my departure from Yorkshire had been sad and distasteful and I shall never forget a personal touch from the captain, Barry Wood. I had known Woody since his days as a Yorkshire Colt in the early 'sixties and from the opposition ranks I had then watched the great transformation as he developed into a very good player, first with Lancashire and then with Derbyshire. I was glad to find he had lost none of his amusing characteristics (while becoming a pretty tough captain with some good ideas) and he frequently made me laugh out loud, even in the middle of an innings. In the course of a casual conversation before the season started I asked if Derbyshire held a pre-season lunch for the players as we had always done in Yorkshire. He replied thoughtfully, 'No, but it's a damned good idea. Leave it with me.' I thought no more about it until Barry gleefully announced that he had persuaded the chairman to put on a lunch which duly took place at the Pennine Hotel in Derby. Woody was a bit like a cat on hot bricks, restless but secretive and occasionally enjoying a quiet chuckle to himself. Several times he was in whispered conversation with the head waiter but he wouldn't say what was afoot. Finally, with the meal finished and everyone waiting to see if there were any speeches, Barry had another word with the head waiter. Music struck up, curtains were drawn slowly apart and there we saw – a stripper! Good old Woody! Only he could have dreamed it up and I couldn't help wondering what the president would have thought. Or, indeed, what the Yorkshire committee would have said if we had introduced a stripper at Headingley.

So at least I was off to a laughing start with my new county and that was therapeutic in itself. It was a change to play most of my cricket in front of smaller and very much less vociferous crowds, but I came to enjoy it as much more relaxing. Yet at the end of the day my job was still the same – to go out there and score runs and to entertain. It's so much easier to entertain when you are enjoying it yourself.

It was also something of a change to go into a side on the crest of a wave after just winning the Nat West Trophy in its first year, and certainly there seemed all the makings of another successful year but things just ran away from us at important moments. We finished up halfway in everything, more or less, but there was much to impress me, seen at close quarters for the first time. Bob Taylor is just incredible, incomparably the best wicket-keeper in the world. Outside Test cricket where obviously he is unproven, Peter Kirsten must be the best batsman playing the game, and John Wright will certainly get into my top half-dozen openers in world cricket. It's a bit of an education to play alongside chaps like those two because they get on with their game so well. Their technique is good, they improvise well and they score a lot of runs on a wicket at Derby which is not ideal for scoring because it is very slow and low. Geoff Miller is a thoroughly good lad (though I wish he'd get that damned first hundred!) and certainly the best batsman of the three off-spinners picked for the Australian tour of 1982–83. But the player who has impressed me most from a cricketing point of view is Dallas Moir, the slow left-armer from Aberdeen who was recommended to the county by Brian Close, as manager of Scotland's Benson and Hedges team. If Closey recommends a player you take notice, and I watched this chap improve by the hour. He got nearly 80 wickets in a season which didn't bring a rich harvest for spinners generally.

I still had my memories of Yorkshire cricket: some good, some bad, some (at the end) plain awful. Sadly, my lasting memory will be of the greatest of all counties reduced to a squabbling rabble; of squalid, petty argument; of supporters, once the most loyal and sane of all memberships, torn apart by a cult which regarded one man as greater than the club and even than the game itself; and of a committee which made a terrible mistake and didn't try to put things right until it was too late.

Index

Index